D0173596

CULTURE SMART!

ECUADOR

Russell Maddicks

·K·U·P·E·R·A·R·D·

ISBN 978 1 85733 683 2
This book is also available as an e-book: eISBN 978 1 85733 684 9

British Library Cataloguing in Publication Data
A CIP catalogue entry for this book is available from the British Library

First published in Great Britain
by Kuperard, an imprint of Bravo Ltd
59 Hutton Grove, London N12 8DS
Tel: +44 (0) 20 8446 2440   Fax: +44 (0) 20 8446 2441
www.culturesmart.co.uk
Inquiries: sales@kuperard.co.uk

Series Editor Geoffrey Chesler
Design Bobby Birchall

Printed in Malaysia

About the Author

RUSSELL MADDICKS is a BBC-trained writer, translator, and journalist. A graduate in Economic and Social History from the University of Hull, England, he has spent the last twenty years traveling, living, and working in South and Central America, most recently as a Latin American Regional Specialist for BBC Monitoring. A fluent Spanish speaker, he has made many extended trips to Ecuador, one of his favorite South American destinations, where he has explored the length and breadth of the country both for work and for pleasure. He is also the author of *Culture Smart! Venezuela* (2012) and the *Bradt Guide to Venezuela* (2011). You can follow him on Twitter @EcuaTravelGuide.

The Culture Smart! series is continuing to expand.
For further information and latest titles visit
www.culturesmart.co.uk

The publishers would like to thank **CultureSmart!**Consulting for its help in researching and developing the concept for this series.

CultureSmart!Consulting creates tailor-made seminars and consultancy programs to meet a wide range of corporate, public-sector, and individual needs. Whether delivering courses on multicultural team building in the USA, preparing Chinese engineers for a posting in Europe, training call-center staff in India, or raising the awareness of police forces to the needs of diverse ethnic communities, it provides essential, practical, and powerful skills worldwide to an increasingly international workforce.

For details, visit www.culturesmartconsulting.com

CultureSmart!Consulting and **CultureSmart!** guides have both contributed to and featured regularly in the weekly travel program "Fast Track" on BBC World TV.

contents

contents

Map of Ecuador

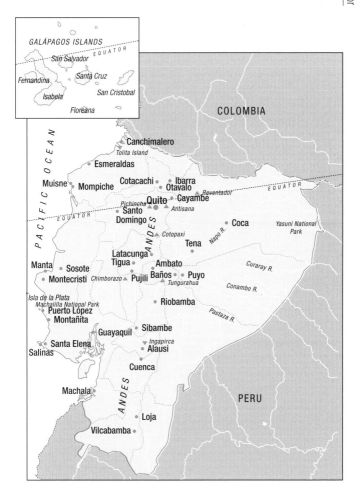

introduction

Ecuador may be the fourth-smallest country in South America, but this compact Andean nation punches above its weight in terms of diversity, from its world-class wildlife and bird-watching opportunities to a geographical landscape so varied that it has been described as a microcosm of every micro-climate found in South America.

Squeezed between Colombia in the north and Peru in the south, Ecuador is named for its location on the Equator. It has some of the highest and most active volcanoes in the world; steamy Amazon jungles in the east; a Pacific coast dotted with fishing villages and beach resorts; and, out to sea, the jewel in the country's crown—the fabled Galápagos Islands, named after giant tortoises that can live for more than 150 years, and where the young Charles Darwin first had the seed of an idea that germinated into the Theory of Natural Selection and Evolution. All this diversity makes Ecuador a magnet for tourists, mountain trekkers, volunteers, and increasing numbers of US retirees looking for a warm, culturally interesting, economical, and safe place to spend their retirement dollars.

Ecuador has a multiethnic population that reflects a unique blend of cultures, from traditionally dressed mountain peoples whose ancestors inhabited their highland villages before the arrival of the Incas to the Afro–Ecuadorians of Esmeraldas and the Chota Valley and the tribal peoples of the Amazonian rain forest. Ecuadorians are proud, friendly, hospitable, and hardworking, but to understand the culture in any depth you need to know the complex historical divisions between the highlands and the coast, and the rigid class and racial discrimination that has dominated the country's history.

Now the country is booming, due in great part to the policies of President Rafael Correa, first elected in 2006, with high oil prices benefiting this OPEC nation, and investment in tourism seeing visitor numbers sharply rising. Determined to forge ahead with his "Citizen's Revolution," Correa has brought political stability to a nation that had seen seven presidents come and go in the turbulent years between 1996 and 2006. A US-educated economist who follows a similar line to Venezuela's Hugo Chavez and Bolivia's Evo Morales, Correa has funded a massive infrastructure program by defaulting on the nation's debt, renegotiating oil contracts, making the tax system work, and turning to China for loans.

Fixing roads, building schools, and extending social security protection and poverty-reduction programs have endeared the president to the poorest in Ecuadorian society. His attacks on bankers, oligarchs, and rich media owners have infuriated the moneyed elite, who portray him as a brash populist who is rude and dismissive of his critics and interested only in remaining in power.

Culture Smart! Ecuador takes you beyond the usual descriptions of where to go and digs deeply into the heart of this multilayered, multiethnic nation to provide you with an insider's view of the people, the history, the food, the culture, and an understanding of how Ecuadorians do business, make friends, and meet members of the opposite sex.

10

Key Facts

Official Name	República de Ecuador	
Capital City	Quito	Pop. 2.239m Altitude 9,350 ft (2,850 m)
Main Cities	Guayaquil (pop. 2.35m); Cuenca (330,000); Ambato (329,850); Santo Domingo (322,00)	
Area	99,706 sq. miles (258,238 sq. km)	Ninth-largest/ fourth-smallest country in South America
Population	15,439,429 (2013 estimate)	
Ethnic Makeup	71.9% Mestizo (mixed race); 7.4% Montubio; 7.2% Afro–Ecuadorian; 7% Indigenous; 6.1% White (2010 Census)	
Geography	Straddles the Equator in NW South America. Borders Colombia in the north, Peru in the south and east; long Pacific coast on the west	Diverse terrain. Mountains; snow-covered volcanoes; cloud forests; tropical rain forests; major river systems; coastal lowlands; beaches; islands
Climate	Coast dry and hot with rainy season downpours; rain forest hot, wet, humid; mountains cool, temperate. and low of 48.5°F (9° C)	Quito temperatures spring-like year-round. Average high of 67°F (19.5° C)
Seasons	Seasons vary with altitude. Dry months Sep.–Nov. on coast; Jun.–Oct. in highlands; Nov.–Mar. in the Amazon.	Sunrise (± 6:00 a.m.) and sunset (± 6:00 p.m.) change little throughout year.

Life Expectancy	Men 73; women 79	Infant mortality: 18 deaths per 1,000 live births
Languages	Official language: Spanish. 12 indigenous languages. Quechua and Shuar officially recognized in 2008 Constitution	
Literacy Rate	97%	
Religion	80% Roman Catholic; 11% Protestant/Evangelical; 1% Jehovah's Witness; 8% indigenous beliefs/other. Protestants have made significant gains in recent years.	
Government	Democratic Republic with a unicameral National Assembly elected every four years. President is chief of state and head of government, elected every four years. There are 24 provinces, each with an administrative capital.	
Media	Newspapers: *El Comercio*, *El Universal*, *Hoy*. *El Telegrafo* in Guayaquil is state-run. *Vistazo* is a popular magazine.	6 private TV channels, incl. Ecuavisa and Teleamazonas. 4 state TV channels, incl. Gamavision
Currency	US dollar (US $)	
GDP Per Capita	$ 8,800	
Electricity	110 volts, 60 Hz	European appliances need adaptors.
Internet Domain	.ec	
Video/TV	NTSC–DVD Zone 4	
Telephone	International dialing code 593	City codes: Quito 2; Guayaquil 4; Galápagos 5; Cuenca 7
Time Zone	UTC/GMT -5:00 hrs	

chapter one

LAND & PEOPLE

GEOGRAPHY

Covering 109,483 square miles (283,561 sq. km), Ecuador is the smallest of the Andean countries and the fourth-smallest country in South America, similar in size to the US state of Colorado. It straddles the Equator on South America's western coast, and the long Pacific coastline stretches some 1,452 miles (2,337 km) from the border with Colombia in the north to the border with Peru in the east and south. Off the coast lie the Galápagos Islands.

Ecuador has a diverse geographic terrain that includes Andean mountains, active and inactive volcanoes, montane valleys, cloud forests, steamy Amazon jungle, arid deserts, and its long Pacific coast. The four main geographic regions are the Sierra, or Andean highlands, running from north to south in the center of the country; the Costa, or Pacific coast in the west; the Oriente, or Amazon region, in the east; and the Galápagos Islands.

La Sierra—the Andean Mountains and Valleys

The Ecuadorian Andes run from north to south along two mountain chains known as the Eastern Cordillera and the Western Cordillera. Between them is a high intermontane valley. The highest peaks are the volcanoes Chimborazo, at 20,702 feet (6,310 m), Cotopaxi, at 19,347 feet (5,897 m), and Cayambe, at 18,996 feet (5,790 m). Ecuadorians are proud to point out that, due to the bulge at the equator, Chimborazo is the farthest point on the planet from the

center of the earth, making it technically higher than Mount Everest. One of the most active volcanoes is Tungurahua at 16,456 feet (5,016 m), which rises above the popular tourist town of Baños, named for its sulfurous hot springs, which are believed to have health-giving properties.

The capital, Quito, is in a mountain valley at 9,350 feet (2,850 m) above sea level. Overlooking Quito are the twin peaks of Guagua Pichincha, at 15,696 feet (4,784 m), and Rucu Pichincha, at 15,413 feet (4,698 m).

La Costa—the Pacific Coast

The Costa comprises a wide coastal belt that runs from the border of Colombia to the border of Peru, and from the sea to the foothills of the Andes. In the north, areas of tropical rain forest are maintained by the high rainfall associated with the warm waters of the El Niño current from Panama. Farther south, cattle ranching and the agricultural production of bananas have led to extensive deforestation that has seen 98 percent of the native forest cut down. What remains of the rain forest, cloud forest, and dry forest in the mountains along the coastal strip is part of the endangered Tumbes-Chocó-Magdalena biodiversity hotspot, which provides microclimates for hundreds of endemic bird species, rare howler and spider monkeys, and other mammals. Private reserves aim to preserve these last remaining areas of native forest.

In the south, scrub and deserts predominate on the southern coast due to the drying effects of the Humboldt Current, which brings cold, nutrient-rich water from southern Chile up to the Equator. Although it provides abundant stocks of sardines, anchovies, and mackerel, these are prone to periodic depletion caused by the El Niño phenomenon. Guayaquil is the dominant city on the coast and the country's largest port. All along the coast there are beach resorts catering to locals and foreign tourists.

El Oriente—the Amazonian Rain Forest

The east of Ecuador is known as El Oriente, a swath of hot and humid rain forest that covers nearly half of the country and teems with tropical wildlife and birds. It is also home to indigenous people, such as the Quechua-speaking Kichwa, who have been integrated into Ecuadorian society, and the remote Waorani who, despite the encroachment of loggers and oil companies, live very much as they did before the arrival of Europeans.

Running through this heavily forested region are major rivers, such as the mighty Napo, which starts as meltwater on the glaciers of volcanoes like Cotopaxi, Antisana, and Sichulawa, and is fed by the Coca River before joining the Amazon in Peru. In the lower Oriente around Puyo, the Pastaza River feeds into the Marañón River in Peru.

Oriente is home to Ecuador's most important nature parks, such as the Yasuni National Park, a designated UNESCO Biosphere Reserve that has been described by ecologists as the most biologically diverse spot on the planet. However, the region is also the location of the country's principal oil reserves, and past drilling of oil wells around Lago Agrio, the building of access roads into the region, and the poisoning of rivers with inadequately treated toxic waste and oil spills has shown how environmentally damaging oil extraction can be for these fragile forest environments.

The Galápagos Islands

The eighteen main islands and fifty or so smaller islets of the volcanic Galápagos archipelago have been described as a living museum and a showcase of evolution. Located some six hundred miles (1,000 km) off the mainland in the Pacific

Ocean, the islands were formed from undersea volcanic eruptions from 8 million to 3.5 million years ago and cover an area of 3,090 square miles (8,010 sq. km).

The Galápagos Islands are home to plants, animals, and birds that evolved in isolation, making the archipelago a "natural laboratory of evolution." Charles Darwin featured their extraordinary diversity in his book *The Voyage of the Beagle*, which recounts his 1835 visit to the Galápagos, and he later used the example of adaptations among finches on the different islands to support his Theory of Evolution and Natural Selection. In 1978 the Galápagos was the first place on the planet to be declared a UNESCO World Heritage Site.

English pirates used the islands to hide out when targeting Spanish treasure ships, and early maps feature the English names for the islands. They were officially annexed by Ecuador on February 12, 1832. The main industry is tourism, and 170,000 visitors flock here each year to marvel at the blue-footed boobies, marine iguanas, tame sea lions, and giant tortoises. Recent fears that the growth of tourist infrastructure on the main islands of San Cristobal, Santa Cruz, Floreana, and Isabela, including the growing number of cars, is having an increasingly negative impact on the wildlife have prompted measures aimed at regulating the numbers. Most tourists still choose to visit the islands on cruise boats, which maximizes the number of islands and dive sites that can be seen.

CLIMATE

Despite its position on the Equator, Ecuador does not have typically tropical weather throughout the country as the climate depends on altitude. In the Sierra, the intermontane valleys enjoy a year-round spring, while in high mountain villages nights can dip below freezing. It's easy to get sunburned in Quito, even when the days are cloudy, due to the altitude. The coast is hot, and the jungles of Oriente are hot and humid.

Rainfall depends on the season. The dry season (*temporada seca*) is also known as *verano* (summer) and the rainy season (*temporada de lluvia*) is also known as *invierno* (winter). However, seasonal variations in rainfall depend on the region. In the Sierra, the rainy season generally runs from October to April. However, the weather is never predictable and citizens of the Sierra say you can experience four seasons in one day in the mountains. Even in the dry season you should pack for the occasional shower or cold spell.

In the rainforests of the Oriente, high rainfall and humidity are the norm and there is little change in temperature throughout the year, although nights can get very cool. The rainy season is generally from April to September, but it can rain on any day.

The coastal area around Guayaquil can be very hot and humid in the rainy season from December to May. Esmeraldas in the north receives more rainfall than the southern coast, and the central coast is sometimes blanketed in a thick, damp mist, known as *garúa*.

In the Galápagos, the cooler dry season runs from July through December and is also known as the *garúa* season, with mist coming down from the higher elevations to the coast. In the warm, wetter season from January to June there is very little rainfall on the low-lying coasts, and sunshine and blue skies are typical. Temperatures on the beaches range between 84°F (29°C) and 59°F (15°C).

THE EQUATORIAL BULGE AND DARWIN'S FINCHES

Ecuador provided the world with some major scientific breakthroughs in the eighteenth and nineteenth centuries, one of which gave the country its name.

In 1735, the French Geodesic Mission set out for South America to find out if the Earth was round, or if it bulged out at the middle like a squashed ball—a theory put forward by the great English physicist Sir Isaac Newton (1642–1727). Led by the French mathematician and naturalist Charles Marie de La Condamine (1701–74), the mission planned to measure degrees of latitude on the Equator and compare them to measurements from Europe and the Arctic. La Condamine was accompanied by the Astronomer Louis Godin, mathematician Pierre Bouguer, and two Spanish naval officers.

The expedition was planned for three years, but took nearly ten. Along the way, the scientists were exposed to great hardships, extreme cold, and fevers, and the expedition's surgeon, Jean Seniergues, was stabbed to death by a mob at a Cuenca bullfight.

However, by triangulating the peaks of Andean volcanoes and mountains near Quito with points on the ground along a 215-mile line to the city of Cuenca, the French scientists eventually proved that one degree of latitude was shorter at the Equator, proving Newton's theory that the Earth did indeed bulge out at the middle. Their discovery led to the production of the first accurate maps. It was La Condamine's adventure-filled account of his travels that firmly associated the Audiencia de Quito with the "Land of the Equator" that he so thrillingly described, and led eventually to the naming of the first republic in 1830 as Ecuador.

Inspired by the French expedition, the Prussian naturalist and explorer Alexander von Humboldt (1769–1859) arrived in Quito in 1802 following a trip that took him from Venezuela through Colombia. A keen geologist and climber, he attempted to reach the snow-capped summit of Chimborazo, but only reached 19,286 feet (5,878 m) before becoming affected by altitude sickness, which he correctly guessed was linked to oxygen deficiency. Passionately interested in the social conditions of the people he encountered on his travels, Humboldt marveled that "Ecuadorians sleep peacefully amid smoking volcanoes, live in poverty atop riches, and are made happy by sad music." He gave his name to the cold Humboldt Current that sweeps up from Chile creating the arid deserts of Ecuador's south coast, and dubbed the mountainous area around Chimborazo "The Avenue of the Volcanoes." Chimborazo remained unconquered until the British climber Edward Whymper made it to the top in 1880.

On September 15, 1835, the British naturalist Charles Darwin (1809–22) arrived in the Galápagos Islands as part of a five-year research trip around the world on board HMS *Beagle*. He was immediately struck by the tameness of the local wildlife, and during the five weeks he studied the archipelago he noted differences between the plants and animals on islands so close to each other. But it was only later, after much study of the collections he made there, that he came to the realization that the differences among the many finches he found on the islands were adaptations to different conditions over time. His short visit would lead, years later, to his groundbreaking book *On the Origin of Species*, the basis for the modern Theory of Evolution.

PEOPLE

Ecuador's people are as diverse as the country's geography. According to the 2010 Census, some 71 percent identify themselves as *mestizos* (mixed race), a legacy of the Spanish conquest. Only 6.1 percent class themselves as *blancos* (white), but they make up the majority of the rich elite in business, land ownership, and politics. They generally claim Spanish descent, although later European immigrants have married into the elite, particularly since the 1940s. Surprisingly, given the strong presence of indigenous Ecuadorians in the highlands, Quito, Santo Domingo, and the Amazon region, only 7 percent of

Ecuadorians describe themselves as indigenous. There are some twenty-seven indigenous groups in the country, including the Andean Quichua and Amazonian Kichwa. The Cofán, Siona, Tetete, Secoya, Waorani, Shuar, Achuar–Shiwiar, and Záparo are found in the Amazon areas of El Oriente, and the Cha'palaachi (Cayapa), Tsachila (Colorado), and Awa indigenous groups are located in the coastal lowlands. A further 7.4 percent describe themselves as *montubios*, a word used for the mixed-race people who live outside the main towns and cities along the coast. The 7.2 percent who describe themselves as Afro–Ecuadorian are descendants of African slaves who were concentrated in two areas: Esmeraldas Province on the coast and the Chota Valley in Imbabura Province.

There are large communities of Colombians living along the border and in Santo Domingo de los Tsachilas, Peruvians in the south, and a small but growing number of Cubans in the main towns and cities.

There is a small but significant Lebanese community, known as *Turcos* (Turks), because they first arrived at the end of the nineteenth century, when Lebanon was part of the Ottoman Empire. They have provided the country with three presidents, including Abdalá Bucaram and Jamil Mahuad. A four-thousand-strong Jewish community, based mainly in Quito and Guayaquil, dates from the 1930s, when Jews fleeing persecution in Nazi Germany took shelter here.

A BRIEF HISTORY

There is insufficient space to do full justice to the epic sweep of Ecuador's pre-Columbian past and its complex history, including as it does the blood-soaked struggle of Atahualpa—a Quito-born son of the Sapa Inca—for control of the Inca empire; the brutal Spanish conquest that brought a forced conversion of the indigenous population to the Roman Catholic religion; and the wars of independence that led to the birth of Ecuador as a nation. Those momentous events were followed in the nineteenth century by an internal battle for control between Quito and Guayaquil, and a largely unsuccessful external battle to protect the borders from the depredations of the country's more powerful neighbors Colombia and Peru. On the cusp of the twenty-first century there was more turmoil, with indigenous uprisings as an oppressed underclass took to the streets to express their demands for a more inclusive and equal society; military coups as the generals asserted their will; and political upheaval as presidents failed to finish their terms. A succession of financial crises led to a mass migration of working-age Ecuadorians and continued political unrest until 2006, when President Rafael Correa was first elected, which ushered in a new period of political stability, rising living standards, a boom in tourism, and the arrival of thousands of US expatriates seeking a retirement haven.

Earliest People

The long-held theory that hunter-gatherers from Siberia populated the Americas after crossing the Bering Strait at the end of the last Ice Age, around 11,500 years ago, has been largely revised. Human footprints preserved in volcanic ash in Valsequillo, Mexico, date back 35,000 years, and other archaeological finds suggest even earlier dates. Recent DNA research indicates that the Americas were populated in several waves of migration over many years, and some of the first Americans probably used small boats to travel down the Pacific coast.

In Ecuador, the earliest known settlements belonged to the Las Vegas culture, which occupied several sites along the coast in present-day Santa Elena some ten thousand years ago. They subsisted on hunting, fishing, and foraging, and there is evidence in Santa Elena of the earliest examples of cultivated plants, such as the gourd tree and maize. The most dramatic discovery in the region was a cemetery of about two hundred burials, including a grave in which two skeletons were found in what looks like a tender embrace. Dubbed "*los Amantes de Sumpa*" (the Lovers of Sumpa), they are a major draw to a small museum built on the site.

The Valdivia Culture group (3,500–500 BCE) is the oldest ceramic civilization found in Ecuador, and is known for "Venus" or "Earth Mother" figurines, depicting naked, sometimes pregnant, women. Often intentionally broken, they may have been used in fertility and healing rituals. In the 1960s, Ecuadorian archaeologist Emilio Estrada noticed strong similarities between the ceramics of Valdivia and the Jomon culture of Kyushu Island in Japan. Estrada's theory that Japanese fishermen had "discovered" the Americas four thousand years before Columbus is no longer seen as credible.

Other important formative cultures include the Machalila (1,500–1,000 BCE) from Manabí and Santa

Elena, who practiced cranial deformation in childhood, perhaps to identify an elite class; and the Chorrera (1,300–300 BCE), who made fine red pottery and used the shell of the *spondylus* (thorny oyster) as a form of

currency to trade with other groups. La Tolita (600 BCE–400 CE), focused principally around Tolita Island in Esmeraldas, is named after the *tolas* (burial mounds) found here. A center for religious ceremonies possibly linked to ancestor worship, the island was home to artisans producing exquisite figurines and masks made of gold and platinum. The gold funerary mask of the Sun God in the Museo Nacional del Banco Central de Ecuador in Quito comes from Tolita.

Life Before The Incas

Before the arrival of the Incas, the Manteños, and the Caras, or Caranqui, were large tribal groups that emerged on the coast. The Caras built an impressive ceremonial site at Cochasqui, with fifteen large earth pyramids, that dates back to about 850 CE and continues to awe visitors today. Remains of hilltop fortresses called *pucaras* have also been excavated. Later, the Caras merged with the Quitus from the highlands to create a tribal confederation known as the Shyris. It was the Quitus who gave their name to Quito, a city named by the Incas.

Another group that had extensive trade routes between the coast and the sea was the Yumbos, whose ceremonial site at Tulipe, in the cloud forests outside Quito, is only being slowly revealed by archaeologists today. Other groups named by the Spanish chroniclers were the Puruhá, and the

fierce Cañari in the south of the country. The Cañari were among the first of these large groups to come up against the armies of the Sapa Inca Tupac Yupanqui. The Incas built Tomebamba (present-day Cuenca) on the site of an important Cañari community, and visitors to Ingapirca, the best-preserved Inca ruin in Ecuador, can still see the Cañari structures incorporated into the sun temple the Incas built on top of it.

The Arrival of the Incas

The Incas traced their history back to Manco Capac, a semi-mythical figure who was said to have emerged from a cave in 1070. Expansion from Cuzco, the Inca heartland, didn't pick up until the reign of Viracocha Pachacutec (ruled 1438–71), who conquered the rival Chimu Empire. It was his successor, Tupac Yupanqui (1471–93), who greatly expanded the empire to the south and north, including southern parts of present-day Ecuador. It was no easy conquest. The Incas' northern advance was held up for more than fifteen years by fierce resistance from

the Caras, but under Huayna Capac (1493–1527), who was born in Tomebamba (present-day Cuenca), the Caras were finally defeated. The last major battle saw a victory for the Incas by the small lake of Yaguarcocha, north of Ibarra. This Quechua name means "Lake of Blood," and

legend has it that thousands of Caranqui warriors and young men were killed and tossed into it until its waters turned red.

With the suppression of the Caras, the Incas stopped their advance at the present-day border with Colombia and set about consolidating their rule, imposing the worship of their Gods Inti and Viracocha, organizing the local tribes in line with their hierarchical structure, and building terraced fields and roads.

LEGACY OF THE INCAS

The Inca Empire was the largest and most sophisticated pre-Columbian civilization in South America. At its height, just before the Spanish conquest, the Incas ruled over some twelve million people and controlled a territory that stretched about 1,500 miles (more than 2,400 km) along the Andes from the border of present-day

Colombia all the way south to the Maule River in central Chile.

The Incas exercised control over the area of present-day Ecuador only for some fifty years, but their impact on the local people went so deep that, five hundred years after the death of Atahualpa, many elements of Inca culture survive.

The Inca language, Quechua, is still spoken by the majority of indigenous people in the Sierra and Oriente, *chicha* beer is still drunk at highland festivals, and Inca gods and goddesses like Inti (the Sun) and Pachamama (the Earth) are still invoked in healing ceremonies.

Plague, Fever, and Decline

When Francisco Pizarro landed in
Tumbes in 1532 with his tiny army of
106 foot soldiers and sixty-two
horsemen, the mighty Inca Empire
had already been decimated by a
deadly disease from the north.
Huayna Capac had only just finished
subjugating the warlike tribes of

present-day Ecuador when he was alerted by *chasqui*
runners of a plague heading toward Quito. Those afflicted
suffered skin eruptions all over the body, provoking fevers,
agony, and death. It is now believed that the plague, which
arrived in the New World with Christopher Columbus,
was smallpox, against which the native population of the
Americas had no natural defenses. Huayna Capac was
himself struck down in 1527, dying shortly after learning
of another great threat to the empire: the arrival of bearded
foreigners who rode on strange beasts and carried sticks
that spoke like thunder and killed from afar.

Pizarro's arrival couldn't have come at a worse time for
the Incas. While in Ecuador, Huayna Capac had fathered a
son, Atahualpa, with a Cara princess, Paccha Duchicela,
from Caranqui. After his father's death Atahualpa fought
his half-brother Huascar in a bloody civil war that pitted
the armies of Quito against the armies of Cuzco and saw
local tribes take sides. The war ended with the triumph
of Atahualpa, but he had little time to savor his victory.
Before he could have Huascar executed and consolidate
his position he learned that Pizarro was on his way to
Cajamarca to see him; instead of sending an army he
gave way to curiosity and agreed to meet the strangers.

Atahualpa Meets Pizarro: Two Worlds Collide

Much has been written about the dramatic meeting
between Atahualpa and Pizarro on November 16, 1532,

and it is one of the key events in the Spanish conquest of Latin America. Although the Spanish numbered only 168 and faced a battle-hardened Inca army numbering many tens of thousands, they had the advantage of steel swords and armor, horses, cannons, and a few harquebuses (small-caliber long guns) against men wearing cotton vests, wielding wooden clubs and swords tipped with obsidian (volcanic glass).

Atahualpa had agreed to attend a feast offered by the Spanish, and arrived with great pomp, carried aloft on a litter by attendants decked out in magnificent tunics with gold and silver ornaments glinting in the sun, and followed by a procession of some five thousand unarmed men. While the conquistadors lay in wait, Friar Vicente de Valverde approached the Inca ruler with a bible and a cross and asked Atahualpa, through an interpreter, to accept Charles V as his sovereign and to convert to the Catholic religion. Atahualpa, unused to a writing system, held up the bible to his ear to hear the great words the friar had spoken of and then cast it down to the ground, angry at the friar's words. Pizarro then forced his way through the throng to the Inca, grabbed his arm, and pulled him from the litter crying "Santiago!"—the call for the cavalry to charge and the cannons to fire into the massed Inca warriors. Trapped in the square, the panicked Incans were easy prey for the better-armed Spaniards. Within an hour Pizarro had captured Atahualpa and killed five thousand of his troops and retainers. The only injury on the Spanish side was a cut to Pizarro's hand.

Atahualpa, thinking he could escape captivity by giving the foreigners the precious metals they so coveted, offered to fill one room with gold and another with silver in return for

his freedom. Pizarro agreed, but before the rooms had been completely filled he realized that Atahualpa was a liability to his plans for conquest. After the defeated Inca Huascar was murdered while being brought to Cajamarca on Atahualpa's orders, Pizarro charged Atahualpa with idolatry and treason, and it was ordered that he should be burned at the stake. As the Incas mummified the bodies of their dead rulers and worshiped them, as a sign of "clemency" Atahualpa was garotted (strangled) on August 29, 1533. Pizarro, with the aid of disaffected tribes like the Cañari, then began to consolidate his control over the Inca Empire.

The last great hurrah of Atahualpa's army came with General Rumiñahui, who hid a huge treasure of gold he was bringing to Cajamarca for Atahualpa's release in the Llanganates Mountains, and engaged the Spaniards in several battles. Eventually he was captured and executed, but not before he had burned the Inca city of Quito to the ground. Despite cruel tortures, he never gave away the location of the Llanganates gold, which treasure hunters seek to this day.

Life Under the Spanish

The present city of Quito was founded by Sebastian de Benalcazar on December 6, 1534, before he went off to conquer Colombia. Francisco de Pizarro's brother, Gonzalo, became the first governor of the city in 1541, and started building the plazas, churches, and government buildings that would see it become one of the finest cities in the Spanish Americas. The religious conversion of the locals was a key goal, as was the construction of churches on top of local sites of worship, to stamp out "heathen" beliefs. The indigenous people not only had to learn a new religion, but also had the backbreaking task of building the twenty

churches and convents that
rose up in Quito from the
ruins of the Inca city. Local
craftsmen were also taught the
artistic techniques that were
needed to fill all these palaces
of worship with devotional
images and statues, so creating
the famous *Escuela Quiteña*
(School of Quito) that by the
seventeenth and eighteenth
centuries was famous for
supplying unrivaled religious

artworks to churches and convents all over South and
Central America.

From the outset, the Audiencia Real de Quito (Royal
Audience of Quito), an administrative unit encompassing
much of present-day Ecuador, was fought over by its two
more powerful neighbors. Established in 1563, it initially
came under the control of the Viceroyalty of Peru, but in
1717 it was transferred to the administration of the
Viceroyalty of New Granada (covering present-day
Colombia).

Almost immediately the indigenous people and the
lands they inhabited were shared out among the Spanish
in a system known as *encomiendas*. Ironically, the Inca
hierarchy that was already in place helped the small
number of Spanish conquistadors to exercise control
over such vast lands, and they quickly introduced new
agricultural projects, from cattle herding to the growing of
wheat and bananas. The only difference from Inca rule was
that the Spanish worked the people harder and gave them
less in return. They also took and shared among them the
Inca nobles' most beautiful wives and concubines, starting
the process of *mestizaje* (racial mixing) that took place
across the Spanish Americas.

AMAZON ADVENTURERS

Ecuadorians will tell you that Ecuador is an Amazonian country—a concept that has led to conflict with neighboring Peru on several occasions and is still a bone of contention. The roots of this strongly held conviction date back to February 1541, when a large expedition set out from Quito, led by Gonzalo Pizarro, to find *El Dorado* ("The Golden One"). Gonzalo sought not only a gilded ruler with riches reputedly greater than the Incas, but also a lost land blessed with cinnamon trees, whose bark provided a spice highly coveted in Spain. Instead, he got lost. His second-in-command, Francisco de Orellana (1511–46), found his way down the mighty river, after setting off in search of food and never returning. One hostile tribe that Orellana found was made up of warrior women who showered their boats with arrows, like the Amazons of Greek myth. The expedition's priest, Fray Carvajal, therefore called the river "Rio de las Amazonas"— a name that stuck. Orellana was the first European to travel the length of the Amazon, and his name lives on in El Oriente, where the starting point of his journey on the Rio Napo is called Puerto Francisco de Orellana, although most locals call it Coca.

The Move to Independence

There were several indigenous uprisings in the Audience of Quito in response to the harsh conditions on the mountain farms and lowland plantations, but it was not until the end of the eighteenth century that a broad independence movement began to take shape.

The *encomiendas* had given way to an equally brutal system known as *huasipungo*, in which agricultural workers were treated as powerless serfs slaving away for their rich Spanish masters. African slaves had also been brought over to work sugar plantations in the Chota Valley, but not in great numbers, and slaves shipwrecked in 1535 had created their own settlements in Esmeraldas.

A rigid caste system operated under the Spanish that placed the indigenous inhabitants at the bottom of society, with blacks above them, *mestizos* in the middle ranks, and a small ruling class made up of the descendants of Spanish settlers, known as *criollos* (creoles). The top jobs were given to *peninsulares*, the Spanish-born officials who oversaw the colonial administration and controlled trade.

On August 10, 1809, a group of *criollos* led by Juan Pío Montúfar rose up in Quito against Napoleon's invasion of Spain. The French emperor had forced Charles IV and his son, Ferdinand VII, to abdicate, and placed his own brother on the Spanish throne as Joseph I. The *criollos* were not at this stage calling for independence, but for the restoration of the Spanish king. After twenty-four days Spanish troops regained control and the conspirators were jailed. Ten were hacked to death by their guards after a failed rescue attempt.

The momentum had started, however, and Quito to this day is known as the "Luz de America" (Light of America) for its part in inspiring other Latin Americans to fight for their independence.

Independence Gained

Another revolutionary government was formed in 1810 that lasted until 1812, but it was not until October 9, 1820, when Guayaquil proclaimed its independence from Spain in a bloodless revolt and set up a revolutionary junta, that Spanish control in the region was seriously challenged.

Meanwhile, the Venezuelan independence fighter Simón Bolívar (1783–1830) had effectively defeated the Spanish royalists in Nueva Granada at the Battle of Boyacá in August 1819 and brought his army down south to support Guayaquil. Bolívar's lover was the Quito-born Manuela Saenz (1795–1856), whom he called *La Libertadora del Libertador* ("The Liberator's Liberator"), for saving his life in Bogotá. A bronze statue of her in full military dress, sword in hand, stands outside the Mitad del Mundo, and her house has been converted into a museum.

On May 24, 1822, Bolívar's most trusted general, Antonio José de Sucre (1795–1830), led the independence forces to victory at the Battle of Pichincha, finally liberating Quito from Spanish rule.

Back in Guayaquil in July, Bolívar had a famous meeting with another great South American independence hero, José de San Martín (1778–1850), who had defeated the Spanish in Argentina, Chile, and most of Peru, and who also wanted to liberate Ecuador. Trumped by a triumphant Bolívar, a despondent and exhausted San Martín surrendered the glory of the decisive battle to free Peru to Bolívar, which took place on December 9, 1824, at the Battle of Ayacucho.

What had been the Audiencia de Quito now became the Departamento del Sur (Southern Department) of Gran Colombia, joining present-day Venezuela, Colombia, Panama, Peru, and Bolivia (named in honor of Simón Bolívar) under one flag.

A New Nation Emerges from Gran Colombia

Simón Bolívar's dream of a federation of Colombian nations did not last long. Venezuela broke away from Gran Colombia on May 13, 1830, and the Departamento del Sur soon followed suit. The name chosen for this new republic was Ecuador, a compromise to the political factions from Guayaquil who preferred the rather insipid Republic of the Equator (a literal translation) to

using the name Quito for the whole county, as it had been under Spanish rule. The first president of the new nation was a Venezuelan independence fighter, Juan José Flores (1800-64), who had married into the Quito elite. Known as the "Father of the Republic," Flores had to contend with many forces trying to tear the fledgling nation apart, and was exiled in 1845 after an uprising in Guayaquil of a group known as the *Marcistas.* Later, another group in Guayaquil ceded part of the country to a Peruvian invasion force in a virtual civil war that ended only when Flores won the Battle of Guayaquil in September 1860.

The rivalry between Quito and Guayaquil hardened into a political battle between the Liberals on the coast and the Conservatives in the highlands from the 1860s onwards. The Conservative President Gabriel García Moreno (1821–75) was staunchly Catholic, and handed the

power for education over to the Church, which made him unpopular, especially with the Freemasons. On August 6, 1875, he was hacked to death on the steps of the Presidential Palace. A plaque on the wall records his last words, "*Dios no muere!*" ("God does not die!")

The violence continued into the twentieth century, when Liberal President Eloy Alfaro was murdered in 1912. Alfaro undid García Moreno's reforms by secularizing education and legalizing divorce. He also finished the Quito-to-Guayaquil Trans-Andean railway, finally linking the highlands with the coast. Ironically, he was arrested in Guayaquil for his part in a coup plot and taken back by rail to Quito, where he was seized by a Catholic mob, dragged through the streets, and murdered.

Military Rule, Invasion, and Oil Boom

The period from the 1920s to the 1970s saw Ecuador transformed from a major exporter of cocoa to a real-life banana republic and, finally, an oil exporter. The 1960s also saw a change to the laws that kept peasant farmers tied to the plantations in conditions akin to slavery.

In the political sphere, instability was the norm, with the military ousting governments on a whim. A great populist and eloquent speechmaker, José María Velasco Ibarra (1893–1979), used to say "Give me a balcony and I will become president." True to his word, he was elected president five times between 1934 and 1968, but only once was able to finish his term, the other four times being deposed in military coups.

After eight years of military dictatorship, the election in 1979 of a progressive president, Jaime Roldós Aguilera (1940–81), was seen as a true return to democracy, but triumph soon turned to tragedy when Roldós was killed in a plane crash on May 24, 1981. Some in Ecuador still maintain that Roldós' death was the work of the CIA.

The period also saw the greatest loss of Ecuadorian territory, when in 1941 fighting broke out between Ecuador and Peru over Ecuador's Amazonian territory.

The Peruvian army vastly outnumbered the Ecuadorian troops on the border and even dropped paratroopers into Ecuador, eventually occupying parts of Loja, El Oro Province, and the Amazon. The resulting peace treaty, known as the Rio Protocol, in January 1942, gave some 77,000 square miles (around 200,000 sq. km) of territory to Peru and left another 38,000 square miles (around 100,000 sq. km) open to dispute because of a lack of clarity over the new borders. Later Ecuadorian governments also challenged the protocol, arguing that it had been signed under duress by a military junta while Peru occupied Ecuadorian territory. Tensions continued to simmer, especially in the Cordillera del Condor, which finally erupted in a brief military conflict in January 1981 known as the Paquisha War. In January 1995 there was a short but bitter clash between the two nations over outposts on the Cenepa River that led to aerial bombing by both sides. A final resolution of the dispute was reached on October 26, 1998, brokered by Brazil, and signed by Ecuadorian President Jamil Mahuad and his Peruvian counterpart Alberto Fujimori.

Political Turmoil, Economic Meltdown, and Dollarization

The 1990s saw further political upheaval with the election in 1996 of the Guayaquil populist Abdala Bucaram, who ran his political rallies like product launches, with music, dancing, and giveaways After promising electors a prosperous future, it soon became apparent that he was more interested in partying than steadying the country's spiraling inflation. Leading the opposition to Bucaram was the Confederation of Indigenous Nationalities of Ecuador (CONAIE), which for the first time brought indigenous issues to the forefront in politics. Strikes and street protests eventually brought down Bucaram, known as "El Loco" ("The Madman"), who was declared "mentally unfit" by Congress and skipped the country, in an unprecedented scenario that saw three presidents in three days.

Then, in 1998, the country was struck by El Niño, a weather phenomenon that whipped up storms and floods, devastating the coast and badly affecting the fishing and shrimp industries. President Jamil Mahuad, faced by falling oil prices, inflation of 60 percent, rising unemployment, a bank bailout, and a freeze on bank deposits, decided in 1999 to take the drastic step of replacing the nation's currency, the sucre, with the US dollar. The decision provoked mass strikes and protests by the trade unions and CONAIE against the deeply unpopular president. Mahuad was forced to resign on January 21, 2000, when the capital was besieged by indigenous protesters supported by Colonel Lucio Gutiérrez and his troops. This short-term coup did not stop dollarization, which was passed by President Gustavo Noboa in September 2000, destroying the savings and purchasing power of ordinary Ecuadorians overnight and creating a massive surge in migration to Spain, the United States, and Italy.

Gutiérrez was elected president in 2002 on a populist platform supported by indigenous groups who expected him to bring in social policies favoring the poor. Instead, he brought in an IMF-sponsored austerity package three years later, prompting a week of mass protests against his policies that led the army to withdraw their support for his government and a Congressional vote to oust him.

Rafael Correa and the "Citizen's Revolution"

After three presidents were ousted in less than ten years, in 2006 the young economist Rafael Correa (born 1963), was elected president, ushering in an extended period of political stability that has also seen economic advances, a rise in the standard of living, and a reduction in poverty and illiteracy. A committed Christian and a declared socialist, Correa has benefited from high prices for Ecuador's crude oil exports coupled with a renegotiation of the country's contracts with foreign oil firms on better terms, and used the income to invest in social policies and infrastructure projects. Committed to social change, he has championed same-sex unions but drawn the line at same-sex marriage, and threatened to resign in 2013 if Congress legalized abortion, which he opposes on moral and religious grounds.

GOVERNMENT

Ecuador is a Democratic Republic with a president, elected by universal suffrage every four years, who is both head of state and head of government and has the power to appoint the vice president and a cabinet of ministers. Over its history Ecuador has been one of the least stable republics in South America, with nearly a hundred governments and twenty constitutions since it declared itself independent from Gran Colombia in 1830.

Rafael Correa, on his election in 2006, set up a Constituent Assembly responsible for drafting a new constitution, which was approved by a referendum in 2008. He was comfortably re-elected in 2009 and in 2013, making him the first Ecuadorian president to be re-elected twice in more than thirty years.

The legislative branch consists of a unicameral Asamblea Nacional (National Assembly) of 137 deputies who are elected every four years concurrently with presidential elections. Under the 2008 Constitution the right to vote was extended to police officers, military personnel, and prisoners. It also extended the vote to sixteen- and seventeen-year-olds, on an optional basis, while for eighteen-to-sixty-five-year-olds voting is compulsory.

The appointment of judges to the National Court of Justice is carried out by a separate Council of the Judiciary, created after a constitutional amendment was approved in a national referendum held in 2011. The changes were made in an effort to speed up the process of removing corrupt and inefficient judges, but critics complain that the Council is made up of allies of President Correa, giving the president too much power over the appointment of top judges.

Local government is administered by the governors of the country's twenty-four provinces. The provincial administrations are run by a governor chosen by the president, and a prefect (*prefecto*) and provincial government (*gobierno provincial*) elected by popular vote. The 221 cantons that are subdivisions of the provinces are run by a representative of the president, and a mayor (*alcalde*) and a municipal council (*concejo municipal*) elected by popular vote.

OIL AND THE ENVIRONMENT

Ecuador's most important source of foreign earnings comes from crude oil, and the government's massive investment in infrastructure projects, health, education, and social programs since 2007 would have been impossible without it. But a long history of oil spills and poorly treated toxic waste water has meant that while oil has brought financial blessings to the country it has also left a legacy of environmental contamination, especially in the pristine jungles of El Oriente, where most of the country's oil reserves are located.

Exploitation of the oil reserves in El Oriente began in 1937, when Royal Dutch Shell was offered a concession, but production didn't take off until Texaco began operations in 1964. By 1970, Texaco had completed the Trans-Andean Pipeline bringing crude from Lago Agrio to Esmeraldas on the coast and production boomed. Given the volcanic nature of the region, there have been significant oil spills over the years.

The Trans-Andean oil spills are compared to the mess left by Texaco between 1964 and 1990 when billions of gallons of toxic wastewater and millions of gallons of crude oil purportedly contaminated an area of 1,700 square miles (4,400 sq. km) that is home to the Cofan, Sicoya, and Huarani indigenous groups. In 2001 Texaco was merged with Chevron, which has been fighting against the damages of $9.5 billion awarded to indigenous groups in a landmark ruling by an Ecuadorian court in February 2013.

THE ECONOMY

Crude oil may be king today, but Ecuador's economic development in the past was tied principally to the agricultural production of potatoes, wheat, and maize destined for local consumption, and cash crops and primary materials for export such as coffee, cacao (cocoa beans), sugar cane, bananas, shrimp, and canned fish. The manufacturing sector, traditionally dominated by textiles and the erroneously named Panama hat, is only now starting to take off as high taxes on imported goods stimulate local production.

Cocoa beans, cultivated since colonial times, were the main generator of foreign earnings from the nineteenth century until the 1920s, when local blight and foreign competition seriously affected Ecuador's position in the international chocolate business. The business is now bouncing back as the international demand for good-quality chocolate has seen local producers like Kallari and Pacari make the most of the country's fine aromatic beans.

The next big crop was bananas. Native to Asia and taken to Africa in ancient times, the first bananas to arrive in the New World came with the Spanish Conquistadors, who brought them from the Canary Islands. Today, Ecuador is the biggest banana exporter in the world, shipping out some five million bananas annually.

Exports of cut flowers have also experienced significant growth in the last twenty years. Ecuador has the advantage of year-round spring-like conditions that are perfect for growing roses in particular.

Large-scale oil production began in 1972 in the northern Oriente, and now provides over 55 percent of government earnings. It also, as we have seen, provides the country's main environmental dilemmas. The smallest oil producer in the Organization of Petroleum Exporting Countries (OPEC), Ecuador exports more than a third of its oil to the USA but has been trying to increase the amount it supplies to Russia and China. Oil revenue is offset by the lack of refining capacity, which means gasoline has to be imported. Under President Correa, the country renegotiated its contracts with foreign oil firms from production sharing to service fee arrangements to increase state revenue.

Ecuador is also looking to exploit other natural resources, including the gas deposits in the Gulf of Guayaquil, and an estimated $2 billion of gold reserves.

Surprisingly, remittances—money sent back by Ecuadorians working abroad in Spain, the USA, Italy, and the UK—are the second-biggest source of foreign revenue. The 2008–09 global financial crisis hit Ecuador hard due to a slump in remittances.

The trauma of dollarization in 2000, which sparked a mass exodus of Ecuadorian migrants, has now helped to stabilize the economy and attract incoming migrants in the form of retirees from the USA. Located mainly in Cuenca, Vilcabamba, Quito, and towns along the coast, many came here after the country was described as "the best place to retire" by *International Living*, an online magazine.

Tourism has seen a boom, aided by a global publicity campaign by the government (#AllYouNeedIsEcuador), focusing on the historic city centers of Quito and Cuenca, adventure tourism, the mainland beach resorts, bird watching and other wildlife tours, and the reactivation of the Guayaquil–Quito railway line. The strategy to continue marketing the ever-popular Galápagos Islands, with mainland destinations as an add-on, has borne fruit, with visitor numbers increasing year after year, reaching 1,366,269 tourist arrivals in 2013.

Much of the recent boom in the economy has been driven by the government, which has invested in infrastructure, expanded the public sector, and renegotiated foreign debt payments (the president even defaulted on $3.2 billion of foreign debt in 2008, arguing that it had been negotiated "illegally" by military governments). Critics have argued that the government has turned its back on traditional markets and lenders and instead indebted the country to China to the tune of billions of dollars in return for future oil sales and the increasing involvement of Chinese oil and mineral companies in Ecuador.

VALUES & ATTITUDES

THE FAMILY

A generation ago many Ecuadorians came from very large families, with five to seven children being common in rural areas and eight or nine not unusual. Nowadays, with greater access to sex education and contraception, the average family size has come down to below three children per couple across the country as a whole. Poor rural families tend to have more children than rich urban ones, although the financial pressures of raising a family in a city mean that low-income families in Quito and Guayaquil are also smaller.

Children typically stay at home while they study at college or university, and leave the nest when they marry. Men often wait to marry until they are in a financial position to start a home of their own, so thirty-something bachelors quite commonly live with their parents. It's also typical to find single mothers living at home and relying on their parents to help bring up their children.

Times were very tough for Ecuadorians in the late 1990s, with falling living standards and an unprecedented mass migration of more than a million people of working age to the USA and Europe in the years leading up to and following dollarization in 2000. From abroad, these economic migrants have continued to contribute to family welfare by regularly sending back money. Until recently their annual remittances easily surpassed the income from bananas and tourism, and were second only to oil exports as an influx of financing from abroad.

ATTITUDES TOWARD RELIGION

The dominant religious influence in Ecuador continues to be the Catholic Church, and over 80 percent of the population define themselves as Roman Catholics. The strong presence of the Church is not surprising, given the aggressive conversion of the indigenous population by Catholic priests that was undertaken alongside the Spanish conquest of the Inca empire, which began in 1532. The Diocese of Quito was established as early as 1545. Under colonial rule, the Church had a virtual monopoly over worship and education, which continued unchecked until Ecuador became a secular state in 1899. If you had any doubts about the power of the Catholic religion in Ecuador, then take a quick stroll around the historic centers of Quito and Cuenca, where church after impressive church—each one decorated with huge gilded altars and religious artworks—reflects the opulent wealth of these institutions of moral instruction and social control. Ecuadorians today continue the Catholic cycle of Sunday services and religious holidays. For some, Catholicism is something they are born into rather than a devout calling—but baptisms, first

communions, confirmations, weddings, and funerals are important milestones in people's lives. Even Ecuadorians who don't go to church will carry images of saints and virgins for "protection," or place a candle in front of a Catholic saint to say a prayer and ask a favor.

Up in the Sierra and in the jungles of Oriente, Catholic rituals and indigenous beliefs have blended to create a syncretic form of folk Catholicism, where a prayer to the Virgin Mary may also invoke the Pachamama (the Inca Earth Goddess) or involve a shaman. Catholic festivals and saints' days are widely celebrated, but aren't always so religious. Many reflect local customs and beliefs that date from before the Spanish conquest, especially in and around Otavalo in the highlands (see Chapter 3).

The Church has also had a powerful political voice, initially supporting conservatism, tradition, and the ruling elite. Then in the 1970s, with the emergence of Liberation Theology, some Church leaders started to engage with pressing social issues, such as the huge gulf between rich and poor in Ecuadorian society, the problem of indigenous land rights, and literacy campaigns. In the meantime, Protestant and Evangelical Church groups such as Southern Baptists, the Church of Jesus Christ of Latter-day Saints (Mormons), Jehovah's Witnesses, and others have made inroads in poor areas of the big cities, especially in Guayaquil, and in indigenous areas in the highlands. There are hundreds of these churches, and they minister to about 10 percent of the population.

ATTITUDES TOWARD DIVORCE, ABORTION, AND SAME-SEX MARRIAGE

In the Liberal Revolution of 1895, led by the anti-clerical Jose Eloy Alfaro (1842–1912), the state became secular and freedom of religion became law, with education becoming the responsibility of the state. Under these reforms civil marriage superseded Church marriage, and divorce became legal, although the social stigma attached to it remains to some extent even today.

The Catholic Church's entrenched opposition to abortion has meant that it is still illegal, unless the life of the mother is threatened or the pregnancy is the result of the rape of a mentally handicapped woman. Only some two hundred legal abortions are carried out each year in Ecuador, and many women endanger their lives by turning to backstreet abortionists. Sanctions are harsh, although seldom enforced, with a one- to five-year prison sentence for the woman and a two- to five-year prison sentence for the abortionist. Human Rights Watch, a non-governmental organization, has said that Ecuador's draconian abortion laws "drive some women and girls to have illegal and unsafe abortions, thwarting Ecuador's efforts to reduce maternal mortality and injury." No change is expected under the presidency of Rafael Correa, a staunch Catholic who has made it clear that he opposes any changes to the law on abortion and threatened to resign if any changes were voted through by Congress: "I will never approve the decriminalization of abortion," he said in 2013, adding, "Our constitution pledges to defend life from the moment of conception."

The Catholic Church has also campaigned to stop the recognition of same-sex unions, but has been less successful. Correa has championed legislation that targets discrimination based on sexual orientation, and has supported same-sex unions, but has made it clear that civil marriage should be "reserved for a man, a woman, and the family." Despite strong objections from Catholic and evangelical groups, civil unions for same-sex couples were recognized under Article 68 of the 2008 Constitution. Legal recognition of same-sex unions does not extend to adoption, however—something for which LGBT groups in Ecuador continue to fight.

MEN, WOMEN, AND *MACHISMO*

Ecuadorians have what might be called an old-school approach to gender relations, where "men are men and women are women." Men should be strong, macho decision makers, and women should keep quiet, look pretty, raise the kids, and cook something nice for dinner.

The different treatment of boys and girls starts young. Boys are spoiled and indulged by their parents and are not usually expected to help in the house. Girls, however, are expected to learn all the skills of running a home.

Men will rarely do anything seen as "women's work," even though tradition   roles of the man as sole breadwinner and the woman as stay-at-home housewife are no longer sustainable when both have to work. The practical result of this is that many women have to shoulder the burden of holding down a full-time job, while still looking after children and doing most of the housework. In a country market the majority of the vendors are women, many with a baby slung on their backs, and maybe other children helping out.

Men are still expected to make the first move in initiating romance. Male gallantry is expressed by holding open doors, paying for everything on dates, leading when dancing, and an effusive line in compliments (*piropos*). Despite this romantic side, some men in Ecuador still cling to the belief that their manliness is linked to how many mistresses they have and how many children they father, which leads to households where abandoned single women are left to bring up children on their own.

The hardest lot falls to indigenous women. A UN report on women showed that the poorest, least educated, and hardest-working women in Ecuador were those who identified themselves as indigenous.

They also had low rates for literacy. Moves to target these disadvantaged groups by the government have had some success in improving the situation, but huge disparities still exist between the lives of the rich elite, with their maids, nannies, and cooks, and the indigenous women who toil away in the small towns and villages of the Sierra.

The Darker Side of Gender Relations

There was a time not so long ago when a woman wouldn't bother reporting domestic violence by her husband because the police and the courts would not take complaints seriously and it was deemed inadmissible for a woman to give evidence against her husband. Women's groups have made strides in fighting for greater protection for women, and there are now family courts that deal with abusive relationships. These courts can issue restraining orders, fine or imprison abusive partners, and forcibly remove them from the family home.

A Vote for Women

In 1929 Ecuador became the first country in South America to give women the vote and the first place they could stand for election. Compare that to Colombia, where women didn't have the right to vote until 1954, or Paraguay, 1961.

REGIONAL RIVALRY

You don't have to spend long in Ecuador to come across an example of the historic and deep-seated rivalry between Quito and Guayaquil. More than just a grudge match between the country's two most important cities, the Quito–Guayaquil divide represents a geographic split of Ecuador into the highlands, with a large indigenous population and the country's seat of political power in Quito, and the coast, with a mainly *mestizo* population and the commercial center of the country in Guayaquil. As one observer noted, "Ecuador does its business in Guayaquil, its praying in Quito."

The debate between the two sides can get quite heated. Those from the highlands (known as *serranos* because they live in the Sierra) call those from the coast *monos* (monkeys) and look down on them for being loud, brash, show-offs, and thieves. Those from the coast (known as *costeños*) deride their Andean cousins for being slow, conservative, and hypocritical. Sometimes you hear *costeños* describe people from the Sierra as *longos,* which is just another way of calling them "Indians."

To the outside observer, Serranos come across as polite, reserved, slightly stoic, fatalistic, and soft-spoken, like their Andean neighbors in Peru and Bolivia. *Costeños* live in a much warmer environment, speak fast, are more dynamic, love to dance *salsa*, and are more outgoing. There is also an economic element to the quarrel. *Costeños* claim that they make all the money and pay all the taxes, only for *serrano* bureaucrats in Quito to spend most of the tax money in the Sierra.

There are even some in Guayaquil who see the independence hero Simon Bolívar as a traitor, because he put down a rebellion in the city and incorporated it into Gran Colombia when the locals wanted to go it alone or join Peru. It was pressure from Guayaquil that stopped the country taking the name Quito and opting for Ecuador. In the nineteenth century constant friction between the pro-Church Conservatives in Quito and the anti-clerical Liberals in Guayaquil further polarized the situation, saw politicians assassinated, and on several occasions brought the country close to civil war. Even today Quito and Guayaquil fight over which is the more important— especially when there's a soccer match between them.

NATIONAL PRIDE

Ecuadorians are very proud of their small country and its national heroes. Before the national currency, the Sucre, was replaced by the US dollar on September 11, 2000, the highest denomination bills featured the most important figures from the country's history, such as the presidents Vicente Rocafuerte (1783–1847), Gabriel García Moreno (1821–75), and Eloy Alfaro (1842–1912), the diplomat and essayist Juan Montalvo (1832–89), and the Inca general Rumiñahui (died 1535). Along with the

last Inca emperor Atahualpa (1497–1533), Rumiñahui, who was born in Pillaro in Tungurahua, is considered to be one of the country's first national heroes, especially by indigenous Ecuadorians, because he fought so valiantly against the Spanish after the death of Atahualpa and burnt the Inca city of Quito to the ground rather than let it fall into Spanish hands.

Another source of national pride is the yellow, blue, and red Ecuadorian flag, which, like the flags of Colombia and Venezuela, is based on a design by the great Venezuelan general and revolutionary thinker Francisco de Miranda (1750–1816). The yellow stripe is double the thickness of the other two and symbolizes the abundance and fertility of the land. Blue symbolizes the sea and the sky, and red symbolizes the blood that was spilled in the fight for independence from Spain. The national coat of arms appears in the center, topped by an Andean condor that offers its protection over the nation, and features the snow-covered cone of Mount

Chimborazo and the Guayas River, which links the Sierra with the coast. A sun symbol, flanked by the zodiac signs for Aries, Gemini, Taurus, and Cancer, represents the months of March, April, May, and June, in which important historic events took place. A steamship with a Caduceus symbol as a mast represents the importance of trade to the country.

The most enduring and best-loved sporting hero is the long-distance race-walker and the country's only Olympic medal winner, Jefferson Pérez. But in a nation obsessed by soccer, it's no surprise that Ecuadorians are fanatical about the national team known as "La Tri"

 (short for La Tricolor, because they play in the colors of the national flag). Support has grown immensely since they qualified for their first World Cup in 2002 and reached fever pitch after they got through to the 2014 World Cup in Brazil.

More generally, if you ask ordinary Ecuadorians in the street what makes them proud they will point to the freshness, variety, and great taste of local dishes, especially dishes like soups and *ceviche*. The country's amazing ecological diversity is also a source of pride, including the unique islands of the Galápagos archipelago, with their famous connection through Charles Darwin to the Theory of Evolution.

Most of all, Ecuadorians will tell you that they are proud of the honesty, good humor, and friendliness of their fellow Ecuadorians.

Friendly Insults

Calling people names linked to their physical appearance or nationality is usually considered too personal or rude in the USA and Europe, but Ecuadorians find it endearing, especially when the dimunitive form of the adjective is used by adding -*ito* or -*ita* at the end. Some say that the Ecuadorian habit of giving everybody a nickname was a way of distinguishing between all the kids and cousins called Maria and José in large extended families. A friend or family member will happily greet a girl who's slim with a cheery *Hola, flaquita* ("Hey, skinny girl"). A girl will consider it cute to refer to a rotund boyfriend as *mi gordito* ("my little fatty"). Everything depends on the delivery and the tone of voice. Equally, if you are a foreign visitor to Ecuador and somebody you don't know addresses you as a *gringo* or *gringa* (used to describe somebody from the USA), they are not necessarily being confrontational, unless their tone suggests it.

ATTITUDES TO TIMEKEEPING

The mannered politeness, old-school reserve, and polished shoes of the more well-to-do inhabitants of Quito might create a sense that the Ecuadorian capital is akin to Britain in the 1940s, but it soon becomes clear that you're in South America when it comes to punctuality.

Ecuadorians will rarely arrive at the appointed hour and you are lucky if they are only fifteen or twenty minutes late. This is sometimes blamed on traffic jams and the problems of parking in big cities like Quito and Guayaquil, but you are more likely to hear an excuse like: "Nobody else is on time so we just get into the habit of arriving late." In some situations it is considered quite rude to be punctual, especially when going to somebody's house for dinner, as the hosts will probably not be ready.

For some foreign visitors this flexible attitude to punctuality can lead to frustration—a feeling that many Ecuadorians share. On October 1, 2003, a campaign was launched to tackle this national epidemic of tardiness with a symbolic synchronizing of watches led by the Olympic hero Jefferson Pérez. Suffice it to say that the campaign has had limited success. If you want to insist on something happening punctually you have to emphasize that the given time is *hora británica* ("British time").

RACE, CLASS, AND STATUS

Despite moves by the government to create a more inclusive society and reduce the large economic and social inequalities between rich and poor, Ecuador remains a country where people are judged on where they were born, what they wear, how they speak, the color of their skin, and their last name. Any Ecuadorian will tell you that at the top of the pile are the rich elite of landowners, financiers, agro-exporters, and politicians who are considered *blancos* (whites)—as much for their social status as for the color of their skin. Only 5 percent of the population, they wield huge power and influence.

The middle class—made up mainly of *mestizos* (people of mixed race)—has in recent years grown to about 35 percent (from 14 percent in 2003), and generally aspires to emulate the rich elite by dressing in branded clothing from top international labels, eating at US fast food franchises like KFC, speaking English, having access to cable TV with the latest shows from the USA, and preferring imported over local goods. In Quito, for example, people still try to move to a neighborhood in the more upscale north as soon as they can afford it.

Among the middle and working classes and the poor there is a strong belief that having a lighter skin color opens more doors in life. This leads to expressions like *mejoranda la raza* ("improving the race"), when people marry lighter-skinned partners, and the idea that white, well-off people are *gente de bien* (good people).

At the bottom of the social and economic pile are the Afro–Ecuadorians of Esmeraldas and the Chota Valley, followed by the indigenous Ecuadorians of the Sierra and the Amazon region of Oriente. The working classes and the poor make up about 60 percent of the population, with about 28 percent living on or below the poverty line and 8 percent living in extreme poverty.

Racist perceptions of indigenous people as lazy, slow, and backward are a legacy from Spanish rule, when the indigenous inhabitants of the Sierra were herded together on huge *haciendas* (estates, or plantations) and kept in serf-like conditions by the owners, who lived in luxury like feudal lords. Even after independence there was no change to this system—which was grittily described in Jorge Icaza's 1934 novel *Huasipungo*—until the land reforms of 1964.

Campaign groups have long fought for indigenous rights to ancestral lands in the Sierra and Amazon regions, a greater appreciation of indigenous culture and traditions, and an end to racist attitudes. One of the main indigenous political groups, the Confederation of Indigenous Nationalities of the Ecuadorian Amazon (CONAIE), rose in open revolt in the 1990s, bringing down several governments and opening the debate for a serious discussion of indigenous issues on a national level. CONAIE estimates that, while more than a quarter of Ecuadorians belong to indigenous groups, only 7 percent identified themselves as indigenous in the 2010 Census because of negative attitudes to indigenous people.

ATTITUDES TOWARD FOREIGNERS

Ecuadorians are generally very welcoming to foreigners and are supportive of the government's efforts to promote tourism. Ecuador is a country that until recently saw more people leaving than arriving. The late 1990s saw a period of hyperinflation and negative growth that culminated in the decision to dollarize the currency in the year 2000. Many people's life savings were lost overnight, and the steady trickle of Ecuadorians heading to the USA and Europe in search of work became a flood. Mass migration created a positive image of foreign countries generally, because whole families benefited from the remittances sent back, but incidents of poor treatment of some Ecuadorians in Spain, which were widely reported in the local media, served only to reinforce a negative image of the Spanish that remains from the Wars of Independence and the oppression of indigenous Ecuadorians.

In the USA, the destination for the majority of Ecuadorian migrants, regular crackdowns on illegal immigrants also resonated in Ecuador, only adding to the impression of the USA as an arrogant interventionist state trying to impose its will as the most powerful country in the region. In the 1960s, opposition to the USA saw left-wing and nationalist groups embrace a "Yankee, Go Home" attitude. President Correa played up to this trend when he refused to extend the agreement that allowed the US Air Force to use the base at Manta. He also snubbed the US government in 2012 when he offered asylum to the Wikileaks founder Julian Assange in the Ecuadorian embassy in London, and later to former US intelligence contractor Edward Snowden.

Citizens from the USA or Spain will rarely find themselves affected by the legacy of conquest or geopolitical spats when traveling or living in Ecuador.

The country is so welcoming, in fact, that Ecuador has been declared one of the best places for US expats to retire to, with about five thousand expats setting up home in Cuenca, Vilcabamba, Quito, Baños, and in towns along the coast.

If there is any prejudice toward foreigners, it is directed mainly at the sizeable communities of Colombians and Peruvians in the country. Ecuador lost considerable amounts of territory to Colombia in the nineteenth century and has been swamped by the large number of displaced refugees fleeing the conflict between the army and guerrilla groups in southern Colombia over the last ten years or so. Colombians have a reputation of being untrustworthy, and of being involved in crime and drug smuggling, but in general Ecuadorians and Colombians get on well. In the south there is a large community of Peruvians, who also have a reputation for scams and swindles.

The latest arrivals to make an impact are Cubans, who come to Ecuador under cooperation agreements between President Correa and the Cuban government that eased the entry requirements. In conservative Quito, the exuberant Cubans have gained a reputation for being loud and brash, and have suffered some of the racial prejudice that darker-skinned Ecuadorians face. In Guayaquil, the Cubans have found it easier to fit in.

chapter three

CUSTOMS & TRADITIONS

Following the conquest of the Inca Empire, Catholicism was imposed on the indigenous people by evangelizing Spanish priests, who incorporated local rituals and beliefs into church ceremonies to aid conversion of their new flocks. The result is a festival calendar that combines the movable feasts of the Church with indigenous customs and traditions, some of which date from before the Inca conquest. There is also celebration of important historical dates, such as the founding of the three main cities—a huge source of local pride—and the nineteenth-century battles that led to independence from Spain and the creation of the modern Republic of Ecuador. Ancient beliefs and customs are preserved in the surviving myths and legends of Quechua-speaking highlanders and Amazonian tribes, in the healing rituals practiced by traditional healers, shamans, and witches, and in the production of traditional handicrafts.

FESTIVALS AND HOLIDAYS

There's a *dia feriado* (public holiday), *fiesta* (feast day or festival), or saint's day celebrated somewhere in Ecuador nearly every day of the year, with some *fiestas* dragging on until the brass bands are too tired, or too drunk, to play any more. At some points of the year it can feel as if they are all running into each other to make one long holiday, especially in the capital, where Las Fiestas de Quito in

November seem to last until New Year. March through June can also seem like an endless round of parties as movable feasts like Semana Santa (HolyWeek/Easter), Corpus Christi, and Carnaval converge into a blur of religious processions, marching bands, street parties, fireworks, and water bombs.

If you plan to travel to any of the major festivals, or follow the crowds to the beach, it's essential to book transport and accommodation well in advance. Bus and plane terminals get quite hectic, and disruptions to the system at these times can leave you stranded in the more remote places, so be prepared for delays. It is also typical for businesses, including government offices, banks, shops, and restaurants, to close down on public holidays, which can be frustrating. When a holiday falls on a Thursday or a Tuesday, many people take an extra day off, known as a *puente* (bridge), to make a longer break.

PUBLIC HOLIDAYS

January 1	Año Nuevo (New Year's Day)
February/March	Carnaval (Carnival)
March/April	Semana Santa (Holy Week) and Viernes Santo (Good Friday)
May 1	Día del Trabajador (Labor Day)
May 24	Battle of Pichincha
July 24	Simón Bolívar's Birthday
August 10	Quito Independence Day
October	Guayaquil Independence Day (First Friday after October 9)
November 2	Día de los Difuntos (Day of the Dead/All Souls' Day)
November 3	Cuenca Independence Day
December 25	Navidad (Christmas Day)
December 31	Año Viejo (New Year's Eve)

OTHER HOLIDAYS AND FESTIVALS

January 6	Día de los Reyes (Epiphany)
January 1-6	Diablada Pillareña
May, 2nd Sunday	Día de la Madre (Mother's Day)
June, 3rd Sunday	Día del Padre (Father's Day)
June 19-22	Inti Raymi, Cochasqui
June 24	San Juan Bautista (St. John the Baptist)
June 29	San Pedro, San Pablo (St. Peter, St. Paul)
June, last week	La Yumbada de Cotocollao coincides with San Juan Bautista and the Solstice
July 26	National Sports Day
August 15	La Virgen del Cisne, Loja
September	Fiesta del Yamor, Otavalo
September 23	Mama Negra de La Merced, Latacunga (First celebration of Mama Negra)
October 1	El Día del Pasillo Ecuatoriano
October 12	Día de la Interculturalidad y la Plurinacionalidad (Intercultural and Plurinational Day)
October 12	Fiesta de los Montubios
November 3	Fiesta del Santo Negro, Canchimalero, Esmeraldas
November	Mama Negra Festival, Latacunga (second celebration of Mama Negra)
November 28–December 6	Las Fiestas de Quito
December 24	Nochebuena (Christmas Eve)
December 28	Día de Los Inocentes

El Año Viejo

On December 31 Ecuadorians bid farewell to El Año Viejo (the Old Year) and greet El Año Nuevo (the New Year) with a big party. All over Ecuador people make or buy papier-mâché figures called *monigotes*, which are filleld with fireworks and ritually burned in La Quema del Año Viejo (Burning the Old Year). Politicians, unpopular public figures, cartoon characters, and anybody in the news are all fair game. Some people write out a list of bad things that have happened over the year so they can be burned with the *monigote*.

The parties are lively events, with dancing to festive music such as *cumbia*, *salsa*, *reggaeton*, and Latin pop. A New Year staple is "*Yo No Olvido al Año Viejo*" ("I Don't Forget the Old Year"), a song from the 1950s sung by Mexican crooner Tony Camargo. Festivities include *viudas alegres* (merry widows)—men dressed up as the Old Year's widow, who roam the streets drinking, dancing, flirting outrageously, and generally enjoying his demise.

At home people prepare a big meal, which is eaten late. Turkey is gaining ground as a festive food in the cities, and *cuy* (guinea pig) is still eaten in some parts of the Sierra.

Cábalas are superstitions aimed toward bringing good luck in the year to come. One popular custom is to wear red underwear to bring love, or yellow underwear to bring luck and money. Some people insist on wearing new clothes, to start the year looking good, and, to bring prosperity, some put $50 in their right shoe, or eat lentils.

It's traditional to eat a grape with each of the twelve chimes counting down to the New Year, and to wash it down with sparkling wine. On the last chime, at the stroke of midnight, there are deafening bangs as the firework-stuffed *monigotes* are consumed by flames in the streets and the parties start in earnest.

Carnaval

Falling on the weekend before Ash Wednesday, Carnaval is traditionally the last blast before the Lenten fast,

so parades and parties are organized all over the country. Expect to get wet, as wherever you go there will be water balloons and surprise soakings. The biggest organized event is in Ambato, where they hold the Fiesta de las Flores y las Frutas (Festival of Flowers and Fruit).

However, Carnaval for many Ecuadorians just means four or five days at the beach.

Semana Santa

Celebrating the crucifixion and resurrection of Jesus Christ, Semana Santa (Holy Week) starts with Domingo de Ramos (Palm Sunday) and concludes with Domingo de Resurrección (Easter Sunday). Ceremonies include the *Via Crucis* (Stations of the Cross), where devotees stage recreations of Christ's sufferings and crucifixion. In

Guayaquil on Viernes Santo (Good Friday) a huge crowd watches as the statue of Cristo del Consuelo (Christ the Consoler) is taken around the streets. In Quito the procession for the statue of Jesus del Gran Poder (Jesus

of Great Power) from the Church of San Francisco attracts thousands of penitents, including *cucuruchos* ("coneheads"), who dress in purple robes with cone-shaped hoods, and *Veronicas,* women dressed in purple with veils. There are also men dressed as Roman soldiers and people dragging heavy wooden crosses as an act of penitence and expression of faith.

Fanesca

Eaten in Holy Week, the filling soup known as *fanesca* is made from *zambo* (gourd), *zapallo* (pumpkin), and chunks of *bacalao* (salted cod cooked in milk). It is holy as well as hearty, and should contain twelve types of grains or beans to represent the twelve apostles. Plan for a siesta after eating *fanesca*, as it comes with slices of boiled egg, *empanadas* (fried pastry turnovers), white cheese, *palmitos* (palm hearts), *maní* (peanuts), and *plátano maduro frito* (fried ripe plantain).

Corpus Christi

Meaning "Body of Christ", Corpus Christi, celebrated on the ninth Thursday after Easter, is a major Catholic holiday. In Cuenca, the holiday is extended for a week and is known as El Septenario. This is a time to enjoy the local sweets and pastries. Huge towers of fireworks called *castillos* (castles) are the main attraction in the evenings. Typical tunes include "Chola Cuencana" ("Mestizo Girl of Cuenca"), a *pasacalle* (passacaglia) by Rafael María Carpio Abad with words by the poet Ricardo Darquea Granda.

In the market town of Pujili, in Cotopaxi Province, indigenous dancers called "*danzantes del Sol*" (Sun Dancers) pay homage to the Sun and the Moon, merging ancient Andean harvest rituals with Catholic imagery.

Wearing masks and elaborate headdresses, they dance through the streets to the music of Andean flutes and drums. The party continues with brass bands playing dance tunes—starting with *sanjuanitos* and ending with *cumbia chichera*—and the crowds dancing and drinking.

Inti Raymi

Taita Inti (Father Sun) was one of the most important of the Inca Gods. Inti Raymi is the Sun Festival, held June 19–22 to coincide with the June Solstice and the maize harvest, to give thanks to the Sun. The main celebration

is in Otavalo and the surrounding towns, with a smaller festival in the archaeological complex of Cochasqui.

Typical events include dancing in the Plaza de Ponchos, the drinking of *chicha* beer and *hervido* (cane alcohol and fruit), and ritual bathing in rivers and waterfalls, particularly the large waterfall in Peguche. A central figure in the dances is Aya Uma, also known as El Diablo (the Devil), a mythical trickster who wears a colorful two-faced mask topped by twelve snakes, representing the ancient wisdom of the indigenous people. Inti Raymi in its present form dates back to the 1970s, when indigenous Otavalans reclaimed the Inca name.

Paseo Del Chagra

Ecuador's mountain cowboys, known as *chagras*, are the focus of the Paseo Del Chagra (Parade of the Cowboys) held on July 23 in Machalila, just outside Quito. The festival dates back to 1877, when Cotopaxi erupted and the local priest went to the base of the volcano with a statue of Jesus. After the priest had held a mass the eruptions stopped, and the *chagras* made a triumphant procession back to town. Cowboys, cowgirls, and children ride horses around town and compete in rodeo events.

Fundación de Guayaquil

July 25, the anniversary of the day the Spanish conquistador Francisco de Orellana founded Santiago de Guayaquil in 1537, is the biggest party of the year in La Perla del Pacífico (Pearl of the Pacific), as Ecuador's largest city is known, The fiesta-loving locals combine it with the celebrations marking Independence hero Simón Bolívar's birthday on July 24.

Yamor Festival

This is the Chicha Beer Festival, held September 1–8, the second major festival in Otavalo. It dates from the 1970s, when local Quechua-speakers decided to revive an ancient tradition of marking the maize harvest in the days leading up to the September equinox (Coya Raymi). *Yamor* is the Quechua name for the *chicha* beer that was reserved for the aristocracy and the Sapa Inca himself. It's made with seven different types of maize and is sacred to the Inca deities Pachamama (Earth Mother), Taita Inti (Father Sun), and Sara Mama (the Maize Goddess). Bands play Andean songs on *rondador* pan pipes, flutes, violins, and guitars, and there are parades, fireworks, and lots of soupy *chicha* beer. One of the highlights is the election of a beauty queen, Sara Ñusta (Princess of Maize).

Mama Negra Festival

One of the most colorful festivals in Ecuador, the Mama Negra Festival in Latacunga, held on September 23–24, is a religious festival in honor of the Virgin of Las Mercedes, but is also linked to the arrival of African slaves in the highlands. The strange cast of characters include El Rey Moro (Moorish King), El Ángel de la Estrella (Angel of the Star), and Mama Negra, played by a local worthy who dresses as a woman, dons a black mask, carries a black baby doll, and follows the processions on horseback. Festival dishes include *champus,* a maize and fruit drink, and *chugchucaras*, a plate of pork rinds. In November the local authorities stage another Mama Negra festival, aimed at tourists, as part of the town's Civic Festival.

Día de Los Difuntos

All Souls' Day, or the Day of the Dead, is held on November 1–2. Families visit cemeteries to tidy up the graves of deceased relatives, celebrate their lives, and share a picnic.

Traditional Day of the Dead food includes *colada morada,* a purple maize drink made with raspberries and other fruit, and *guaguas de pan* ("bread babies"), sweet rolls in the shape of dolls.

Independencia de Cuenca

Cuenca's biggest annual celebration, on November 3, marks the city's independence from Spanish rule in 1820. The party starts on November 1, and includes displays of fireworks, marching bands, processions, craft markets, and live music events. The other big fiesta in Cuenca takes place on April 12 and, rather ironically, commemorates the founding of the city by the Spanish in 1557.

Virgen del Quinche

The small town of Quinche comes alive every November 21 as tens of thousands of pilgrims walk all or part of the seven-hour trail from Cayambe to the shrine of the Virgin, who is the patron of Ecuador. The first church built on this spot dates from 1604, and the wooden statue of the Virgin was carved by Don Diego de Robles, who also made the Virgen del Cisne.

Las Fiestas de Quito

Quito is the party capital of Ecuador in the week of *fiestas* from November 28 to December 6, starting with a beauty pageant to elect La Reina de Quito (Queen of Quito), and continuing with live music events, parades, parties in the parks, and colorfully painted buses called *chiva* buses. For many people the parties continue through Christmas.

Navidad

Christmas is celebrated with masses and nativity plays in churches and schools on December 24 and 25. You will see *pesebres* (nativity scenes) everywhere, from small wooden figures in people's homes to life-sized manikins in public squares. It's traditional in many homes not to put El Niño Jesus (Baby Jesus) in the manger until Nochebuena (Christmas Eve). In Cuenca, they hold an all-day procession on December 24 called El Pase del Niño Viajero (The Procession of the Traveling Child), in which a statue of the infant Christ is paraded through the streets to the music of brass bands and Andean flutes.

Papa Noel (Father Christmas, or Santa Claus) is an increasing presence in representations of Christmas, and many Ecuadorian children now write to him to ask for gifts rather than to El Niño Jesus, as they did in the past. Presents are left under the Christmas tree or *pesebre* on Christmas Eve. Most families eat a late dinner, which may include turkey or chicken in city homes, pork or *cuy* (guinea pig) in the villages, but will definitely be a big sit-down meal with wine, whiskey, beer, or *chicha*.

The other major tradition is to go to church for the *Misa del Gallo* (Midnight Mass), which will be full to bursting in cities and villages alike, with *villancicos* (carols) sung to the accompaniment of fireworks set off in the streets. Día de Navidad (Christmas Day) is the time to open presents, visit family, and enjoy another big meal.

SUPERSTITIONS AND BELIEFS

Ecuador has a rich tradition of superstitions, myths, and ancient healing practices. Indigenous cultures carry on pre-Columbian beliefs that a spirit or soul resides in both animate and inanimate objects, so that trees, mountains, and lakes are living entities, and respect must be paid to them. It is typical to see people in the highlands sprinkling a few drops of alcohol on the floor for Pachamama, the Earth Mother, before drinking some themselves.

Highlanders still believe that mountains and volcanoes are powerful entities because of their association with earthquakes, volcanic eruptions, thunder, lightning, and storms. The Inca temples and shrines on high mountains are no longer scenes of animal sacrifice or *chicha* ceremonies, but it is still held that you ignore these

ancient spirits at your peril. Andean villagers tie red cords or coral beads around their children's wrists to protect them against *mal de ojo* (the evil eye).

Traditional healers, known in Quechua as *yachacs,* are highly regarded and use a variety of techniques, including herbal medicines and ritual cleansing. The ceremonies to cure spiritual ailments like *mal aire* (bad air), or *espanto* (fright) involve incantations, candles, beating with herbs, and blowing smoke or alcohol on patients. In Otavalo and Iluman healers draw out bad spirits with an egg that is rubbed all over the body, or with a live guinea pig that is slapped against the patient and then cut open to reveal where a physical problem may lie.

In big cities like Quito and Cuenca you can find herb stands in the markets where *curanderos* (healers) perform curing ceremonies in cubicles at the back of the stand.

In the jungle regions of Oriente, some tribes are known for their past practice of shrinking the heads of warriors killed in battle so that they could keep the souls that reside in them. The Shuar tribe is famous for these shrunken head trophies (*tsantsas*), and also for the spiritual power of its *uwishins* (shamans), who use the ayahuasca (*Banisteriopsis caapi*) plant in their rituals. Shamans from many different indigenous groups employ ayahuasca ("spirit vine") as a way of connecting with the spirit world, and some offer foreigners the opportunity to experience its powerful hallucinogenic effects in jungle retreats that mix New Age concepts with ancient shamanistic beliefs. Be warned: this has resulted in fatalities.

From Europe comes both a fear of black cats and the superstition that the number thirteen is unlucky—especially when the date is *martes 13* (Tuesday the 13th).

MYTHS AND LEGENDS

In the villages around Chimborazo, the country's highest mountain at 20,564 feet (6,268 m), the locals say that if a pregnant woman is caught out in a storm she will give birth to an albino son of the volcano. They also say that Taita Chimborazo ("Father Chimborazo") is a jealous husband of the active volcano Mama Tungurahua ("Mother Throat of Fire"). When there are thunderstorms in the central valleys the locals say that Chimborazo and Tungurahua are having a domestic argument and throwing angry looks at each other. Chimborazo is also said to have smashed Carihuairazo and El Altar, two nearby volcanoes, in a love struggle over Tungurahua.

Similar tales are told in Otavalo about the volcanoes Imbabura and Cotacachi, which are considered to be protectors of the people and the region. Cotacachi is sometimes called "Mama Cotacachi," or "Maria Isabel Cotacachi," and there are many stories of her relationship with Taita Imbabura.

A stone in Peguche known as "Achilly Pachacamac" is considered sacred by Quechua speakers. Legend has it that Imbabura was fighting the nearby volcano of Mojanda for Cotacachi's affections and threw the stone at him, but it fell short because he had become weakened by his womanizing. Another story from Otavalo tells how an Inca prince and princess who were forbidden to marry threw themselves into the Mojanda volcano and resurfaced as the lakes Cariocha ("Man Lake") and Huarmicocha ("Woman Lake").

TRADITIONAL CRAFTS
The typical fedora hats worn by the highlanders are made in Iluman. Cotacachi produces handmade leather goods. In Agato the local women still weave textiles on back-strap looms, and Zuleta is known for the embroidered blouses worn by indigenous women in the highlands.

Tigua is famous for bright acrylic paintings of Andean village life, folk festivals, and ancient myths. They were originally painted on drums until the 1970s, when local man Julio Toaquisa decided to paint on canvas and a

THE FAMOUS "PANAMA" HAT

The fine, soft, but very strong *paja de toquilla* (toquilla straw) found mainly in Manabí, used to make the Panama hat, was being woven into headgear by indigenous people before the Spanish arrived, and was valued for its ability to shield against rain.

The Panama hat got its geographically confusing name when it became popular with workers on the Panama Canal in the nineteenth century. When Theodore Roosevelt was photographed wearing one on a visit to the canal in 1904, the style went global, and has remained a classic summer essential ever since. The name is such a strong brand identifier that Ecuadorians can't change it now. Signs stating "*Se vende Panama hats*" ("Panama hats for sale") appear even in the village of Montecristi, outside Manta, where the best *superfino* hats are still woven by hand to exacting standards.

President Eloy Alfaro, from Montecristi, made his fortune exporting Panama hats, but the big workshops are now in Cuenca, where the Museo del Sombrero de Paja Toquilla shows how the hats are made.

A Panama hat is a "must-buy" in Ecuador, whether you haggle over a US $4 straw sold at a Quito market or head for Quito's Plaza San Francisco and pay $400 for a *Superfino Montecristi*. Light, cool, and hardwearing, the best Panama hats will last a lifetime. The test of quality is the tightness of the weave—so tight that it will hold water. But resist the temptation to try and pass it rolled-up through a wedding ring. Unless it's a good one, this will just ruin it.

whole new style of folk art was born. There are several workshops to visit, where you can see how the paintings are made and talk to the artists about their work.

The *tagua* nut, also called "vegetable ivory," was first carved into buttons in the nineteenth century by German settlers, who closely guarded the secret of what it was and where it came from. Small *tagua* figures are now carved in several places in Ecuador, especially in Sosote, in Manabí Province. A new fad is to dye the nuts with bright colors, polish them until they shine, and set them like semi-precious stones in earrings, necklaces, and rings.

chapter four

MAKING FRIENDS

Ecuadorians have a reputation for being polite and reserved, but, despite an initial shyness toward foreigners, they are naturally friendly people who like nothing more than gathering together in groups to chat, tell jokes, eat, drink, and be merry. As a people who have known hardship and poverty in the past, Ecuadorians make the most of every opportunity to socialize.

THE LANGUAGE BARRIER

The first problem facing a foreigner who wants to make friends is the language barrier. The better your Spanish, the easier you will find it to make Ecuadorian friends, because the majority of people, apart from the foreign-educated elite, or those who work in the tourist industry, know little or no English.

If you don't speak Spanish, or if you don't know a few phrases in Quechua to break the ice, you will be limited to very basic communication. If you're just visiting the Galápagos for a week this won't be an issue, as your guide and the hotel staff will speak enough English for your needs. Equally, if you're in Guayaquil on a business trip, especially if you are visiting firms that have dealings with the USA or the UK, you should have no problems.

If you are living or working in Ecuador, however, you will find it difficult to strike up conversations and make friends. In this case it's a good idea to take a Spanish course, either for a few days, to give your confidence a boost, or for a few weeks, to go beyond the basics.

Quito and Cuenca are recognized as two of the top spots for studying Spanish in South America, because people in the cities of the Sierra have a high level of grammar, speak slowly and clearly, and the classes are good. Many schools offer homestay opportunities, where you sleep, eat, and join in the life of a local family. This is a quick way to pick up a lot of local vocabulary and a good way to make friends. Many people keep in touch with their host families for years after their visit.

If you learn some Spanish and use every opportunity to practice it on the Ecuadorians you meet, you'll soon see how hospitable they can be. They'll go out of their way to teach you new words, and make jokes you can understand so that you'll feel included. Before you know it, they will be showing you how to dance *cumbia*, and stuffing you with local snacks as they teach you how to read the menu.

THE FRIENDSHIP CIRCLE

Most Ecuadorians forge strong friendships at school and among cousins and other family members. By the time they reach adulthood they will have a tight group of friends who are like family, will drop in unannounced for a visit, and be invited to all the important parties and life events. Big families spend a lot of time together, and there are especially close bonds between siblings and cousins. Friends outside the family will generally be school friends from primary school or university buddies, and an outer circle of work colleagues and other acquaintances, such as those who play in the same sports teams.

There isn't the need to find new friends in Ecuador as there is in North America or Europe, where nuclear families and moving out of the family home at a young age are the norm. Most Ecuadorians stay at home until they

marry, and move back home again if they divorce, so their circle of friends can remain quite static. This doesn't mean that foreigners won't make friends in Ecuador—quite the contrary! However, acceptance into an inner circle of trusted friends won't happen overnight.

It's rare to be invited to someone's home. One reason for this is that extended families often live under the same roof, which can make having guests difficult. There is also an issue of class and income. Better-off Ecuadorians have space for entertaining, but poorer people, although used to neighbors and close friends popping in unannounced, prefer to meet new friends out somewhere. In remote villages people might feel their modest home is too humble for a foreigner to visit. You may overcome these feelings over time. The best opportunities to meet a family are at events like birthdays, christenings, and weddings, which are usually held outside the home.

FIRST CONTACT

Ecuadorians enjoy meeting foreigners, and given the chance they like to talk about their country and culture.

The first contact is usually with the taxi driver taking you from the airport, the receptionist at your hotel, or the waiter serving you your first Pilsener beer. Use these opportunities to try out all the Spanish you can muster. Such conversations usually start with where you're from, how long you are staying in Ecuador, and where you intend to visit. The more positive noises you make about Ecuador and the Ecuadorians, the warmer your reception.

However, be wary of someone who comes up to you in the street and starts a conversation for no reason. This might just be a simple hustler looking to make some cash out of a foreigner by showing you to a restaurant or store in return for a tip, but it could be something more sinister, initiated by a scam artist or thief to slow you down or distract you while an accomplice picks your pocket. The best way to deal with somebody you don't like the look of is to act as if you didn't hear them, avoid eye contact, and keep walking. You can politely decline any assistance with a firm "*No quiero nada, gracias*" ("I don't want anything, thanks"), and if that doesn't work enter a store or restaurant and seek assistance from the staff.

MEETING ECUADORIANS

If you are invited to meet other members of your new friend's social circle it's a sign that you've made a good impression. You'll be introduced to the group, and your own circle of friends will start to grow.

If you are working in Ecuador you will find that there is a strong social side to office life. There'll be invitations to eat out for lunch or grab a few drinks after work, a regular parade of birthday cakes, a Secret Santa at Christmas, and even organized sporting events on the weekend, such as softball games or hikes in the Sierra. These are the first steps toward making friends, so take every opportunity that presents itself. If you refuse such invitations you could give the impression that you don't want to make friends and find that no further invitations come your way.

CONVERSATION STARTERS AND STOPPERS

Ecuadorians are polite, and don't want to upset new acquaintances. They will feel happiest having light conversations that focus on positive impressions of their country. Typical questions will focus on your reasons for visiting, where you've been, where you intend to go, what foods you've tried, and a few questions about your family. Steer clear of criticizing the country, the people, the political situation, or the culture, until you know people well enough to have a serious conversation. This is not because Ecuadorians don't criticize their country or don't like to debate the big issues of the day; they do—in fact, you'll find many Ecuadorians who are happy to list the failings of the president or the opposition, lament the terrible traffic jams, and bemoan the high cost of imported goods. But when a foreigner lists the country's failings it can come across as arrogant, especially given the country's love/hate relationship with the USA over the years and the hard times many Ecuadorians experienced in the United States and Europe during the years of mass migration. This is an issue of pride and respect.

Avoid asking about the divide between the people of the Sierra and the Costa unless you know where everybody comes from in your group, as you could open old wounds and create an uncomfortable atmosphere.

People who are polite and keep conversations light and friendly will be seen as *simpático* (nice). People who try too hard to win an argument, or judge Ecuador or Ecuadorians too harshly, will be considered *antipático* (nasty). It's much better to stick to noncontroversial topics such as food, music, places you should visit, and sports— as long as you support the national team, La Tri.

INVITATIONS HOME

If you do get an invitation to somebody's home, then you know you've been accepted into the circle of trust. It's like saying you're one of the family, and is a great honor.

Don't arrive early, or even at the stated time, as your hosts won't be expecting you to do so. As a rule of thumb, aim to arrive about twenty minutes late, and make a point of bringing something to drink. A bottle of good whiskey will always be appreciated, but if you know your hosts drink wine or beer then that's fine too. Ecuadorians are great consumers of sweet snacks, so pastries or fancy biscuits are another suitable gift. Dress casually, but on the sharp side. And expect to dance, even if the invitation is for dinner. Ecuadorians are passionate about music and after a few drinks you'll be invited to join in with a bouncy *cumbia* or swinging *salsa*. There's no pressure to impress—the aim is to have fun as a group.

CLUBS AND ASSOCIATIONS

Foreigners coming to Ecuador for any length of time should seek out some of the expatriate groups that meet up in the major cities, as they will help to ease your way into Ecuadorian society. You'll find expat groups of US and European citizens in cities such as Quito, Guayaquil, and Cuenca, towns like Vilcabamba and Baños, and coastal resorts like Montañita and Salinas.

Ecuador's reputation as a top retirement destination has seen expat numbers rise dramatically over the last few years, especially in Cuenca. The lively expat scene there makes it easy to seek out fellow countrymen, and there are several Web sites offering a weekly roundup of upcoming expat activities and events. Members of these groups will help you to meet Ecuadorians who speak English or like to hang out with foreigners, but it's best to avoid getting stuck in an expat bubble by learning Spanish and seeking Ecuadorian friends to practice with. In towns like Baños and Montañita you only have to track down the microbreweries to find where the foreigners hang out, and Vilcabamba is so small you can't miss them.

In Quito, a good place to meet other foreigners and learn more about the country, the sights to see, and things to do is the South American Explorer's Clubhouse in the Mariscal district on Jorge Washington street, near the corner with Leonidas Plaza. Despite the name, the club isn't just for avid explorers: all are welcome. For a small membership fee you have access to the clubhouse and can sign up for their quiz nights and other events. Another members-only group is Internations, a global expatriate community with some four thousand members in Quito, Guayaquil, and Cuenca, with monthly get-togethers.

SOCIALIZING WITH THE OPPOSITE SEX

Ecuadorians are very romantic—just listen to the lovelorn lyrics of the country's heartfelt songs in the *pasillo* genre. However, to have any success with a member of the opposite sex it's essential to learn the ground rules of the dating game, which can be very confusing for first-time visitors from the USA and northern Europe.

First, a guy can't just wait for girls to come up to him as they might do at home. Ecuador is very much about the man making the first move, just as when dancing *salsa* or *merengue*, where the man leads and the woman follows. For men from countries where women set the speed in relationships, taking the lead may feel uncomfortable, but that's the way it works. A woman who makes the first move in a bar or club may be seen as predatory, or "easy," and attract the wrong sort of attention. Women therefore tend to take a more subtle approach, dropping hints, laughing at lame jokes, and acting "girly" around a man they fancy, while waiting for him to make the first move.

Don't expect to go Dutch if you want a second date. If you invite someone out, you pick up the tab. Suggesting splitting the bill at a restaurant with a date, or buying yourself a movie ticket and expecting her to do the same, is the kiss of death for any budding relationship. Equally, if a woman insists on paying it will hurt an Ecuadorian man's feelings unless he's a *gringuero*—a man who intentionally targets foreign women in bars and clubs.

Basically, a man should treat any potential girlfriend as a princess—he should be romantic and generous, and pay for everything. A woman, for her part, makes the man feel special by dressing up, looking good, and being attentive and affectionate. It's an old-fashioned formula but, despite all the advances that women have made in education and the workplace, it doesn't show any signs of changing.

A typical first date might be a meal at a restaurant, a visit to the movies, or just an afternoon stroll around a shopping mall. You may find that your date turns up with a cousin or friend. Don't be put off—this is just a way of getting to know you before taking any romantic plunge. And it might take several dates to get past holding hands. It's all part of the rather lengthy courting process that is usual in Ecuador.

Mixed Signals

When out in a bar or club, be careful not to misread the signals. If a woman agrees to have a drink or a dance with you, it doesn't mean she agrees to anything else. Close dancing isn't seen as a promise of forthcoming romantic or sexual activity, as it might be in countries where people aren't used to dancing together. Ecuadorians definitely do not see *salsa* as "sex standing up," as you sometimes hear in the USA and Northern Europe. Dancing is just a natural part of any social event in Ecuador, and all generations of an extended family or group of friends will happily dance all night together.

Ecuadorians are complimentary when chatting with friends. Men in particular can be very chivalrous, smiling and paying polite compliments (*piropos*) to a woman, and calling her *mi cielo* ("my heaven") or *mi corazón* ("my heart") just as a normal part of saying hello. A visiting woman shouldn't either jump to conclusions or take offense if an Ecuadorian man spouts a few flowery phrases. He probably does it to everybody.

If someone asks direct questions about your current romantic situation or past relationships, these should not be taken as an indication of romantic interest.

ECUADORIAN PICK-UP LINES

There was a time when Ecuadorian men would show their appreciation of a fair lady passing on the street by reciting a *piropo*, a line of romantic poetry. These usually revolved around stolen hearts, fallen angels, or stars in the sky. You may still hear *piropos* like: "*Cada vez que pienso en ti, una estrella se apagara; te juro que pronto en el cielo no quedaría nada*" ("Every time I think about you a star stops shining; I swear that soon there'll be nothing left in the night sky"), or the classic "*Que alguien llame a la policía— me acaban de robar el corazón*" ("Call the police— somebody just stole my heart"). Foreign women may find such comments ridiculous, but Ecuadorian women quite like these romantic overtures.

Not all *piropos* are sweet and innocent—some are crude. The best strategy is to do what Ecuadorian women do: ignore them completely and keep walking.

HOMOSEXUALITY IN A MACHO SOCIETY

While there are gay-friendly bars and clubs in Quito and Guayaquil, and there is quite an open attitude to homosexuality in beach resorts like Montañita, Ecuador is still a very traditional society in many ways, and public displays of affection between homosexual men or women in the street are not a typical sight.

That's not to say that things are stuck in the past. There are now huge Día del Orgullo Gay (Gay Pride) parades in Quito and Guayaquil every July, which would have been unthinkable ten years ago. The Constitution enshrines the equality of all before the law, no matter their creed, race, or sexual orientation. In Quito there is a vibrant, if underground, gay scene, and making friends is easy. A good place to start is online. There are a number of Web sites listing gay-friendly clubs, and Facebook lists a number of groups, including an "Orgullo LGBTI Ecuador" page with more than three thousand members.

Same-sex marriage is not yet legal, although there is considerable pressure on the government from the LGBT community to bring Ecuador in line with other countries in Latin America.

chapter five

ECUADORIANS
AT HOME

Ecuador is in the process of widespread economic, social, and demographic transformation that is gradually bringing it up to date with the changes that have taken place in its neighbors Colombia and Peru. From a country where most of the population lived in rural areas in the central highlands, as they did, more or less, since Inca times, Ecuador is seeing an accelerated movement of people to the cities as it becomes increasingly urbanized.

HOUSING

Ecuador has a huge diversity among its population, and the places that they live. Quito is roughly divided into north and south, with the poor living in crowded concrete housing blocks in the south and the more affluent in the

new part in the north. In the ultramodern sections of the city, and also in Guayaquil, the rich occupy penthouses with rooms for live-in maids. They overlook shiny new shopping malls, where they can purchase expensive imported goods, including nearly all the brands popular in the USA. Now, after a multimillion-dollar regeneration project in the historic center of Quito, a process of gentrification has started that could see the upper-middle classes moving back into the fine baroque houses that are currently home to multiple low-income families.

In Cuenca, middle- and working-class families live side by side in the well-preserved colonial buildings of the city center, but the pressures of a growing population have seen people with money move out to purpose-built condos and luxury apartments, many of them designed to meet the needs of the thousands of US retirees in Cuenca.

The dusty towns you see in the interior often look the same, with two-story cinder-block homes replacing the wattle-and-daub houses that you still see in highland villages. The only indications of wealth may be the fancy walls and manicured lawns around some of the houses.

One thing you find all over Ecuador, whether on the banks of wide jungle rivers, in the coastal lowlands, or in

the brackish swamps of the Guayaquil slums, are houses built on stilts: the perfect antidote to rising waters and flash floods. In the jungle the walls are often open to the elements; on the coast, in Esmeraldas, they use bamboo. Elsewhere, in the jungles of Oriente, the Waorani continue to build thatched longhouses where several families can hang their hammocks around a central fire.

HOME HELP

You don't have to be rich to have home help in Ecuador. Families who can afford it generally have one or more *empleadas domesticas* or *empleadas de hogar* (maids) living with them to do the chores and cooking and look after the children, with small bedrooms next to the laundry room specifically designed as maids' rooms. You may hear a maid being described as *la muchacha* ("the girl"), even if she is a woman in her fifties. To show respect, younger maids are generally addressed by their first names and older ones by their last names—"Señora Aparicio," for example.

Having living-in servants is seen as an indication of high status, but many families of lesser means have some kind of home help, employing a cleaner for a few days a week. Even in poorer areas people will pay a neighbor to help with washing, cleaning, or childcare as needed.

FAMILY LIFE

Ecuadorians are very family-focused, especially outside the cities, where life is built around the home, and the extended family. Among the indigenous groups in the Sierra and Oriente, affiliation to the tribe is also very important, and they continue to practice ancient traditions like the *minga* (see page 87).

Families used to be big, with eight or ten children not uncommon in rural areas, but now family size has generally fallen significantly, with the average in the cities at about 1.8 children per couple. Children are doted upon by parents and grandparents, and have a godfather (*padrino*) and a godmother (*madrina*)—often an aunt or uncle—who take an active part in a child's upbringing. These *compadres* ("co-parents") are involved in key events in children's lives beyond the baptism for which they are first chosen, and will generally help with the costs and preparations for the celebrations of first communion and confirmation, and the *quinceañera* party.

The general fawning over children, especially babies, extends outside the family home, and foreigners can find it difficult to get used to strangers commenting on their children in the street or on a bus, or patting a child's head. "*Que lindo tu hijo!*" ("Your son is so handsome!") or "*Tu niña es tan linda quiero comerla a besos!*" ("Your little daughter is so pretty I want to eat her up with kisses!"), are typical expressions to show affection to Ecuadorian children. Blonde-haired, blue-eyed foreign children are also likely to attract attention of this kind.

Macho attitudes persist, and some Ecuadorian men believe the number of children they father shows their virility. This can lead to a situation where men have children with multiple partners and disappear, leaving the upbringing of the children to the mothers and their families. This is particularly common in the poorer areas of cities. Grandparents or siblings may take on the raising of a child if the child is orphaned or if the mother can't cope, or sometimes just until circumstances improve.

Although assisted-living facilities exist, it is more usual for elderly relatives to stay with their families. Their pension contributes to the family finances and they may help out with the children, which frees the parents to work.

Life can be a real struggle for poorer parents, who generally have more mouths to feed, less disposable income, and a greater reliance on public healthcare, so every penny counts and the ability to pool resources

from the extended family is crucial. In the past, many children had to work on farms and building sites to supplement the family income, and street kids would survive by shining shoes or looking after parked cars to raise extra cash for the family pot. Nowadays, the number of street kids in cities like Quito and Cuenca has been drastically reduced, although you will still see children working with their mothers as street vendors rather than going to school, and begging has not been entirely eradicated.

However, even the poorest family may invite a visitor in to have tea or coffee and a bite to eat. A popular saying is "*Donde comen dos comen tres,*" which means, "Where there's food for two there's food for three."

THE MINGA

Many indigenous groups in Ecuador have maintained ancient traditions that help to foster strong bonds between individuals and families and the group. One such tradition is *minga*, which in Quechua means "a collective community endeavor." Just as rain forest tribes live in a communal space and hunt and fish and cook together, the indigenous groups of the Sierra work together when it comes to harvesting, planting, or building a house. The work is unpaid, but the beneficiary will provide food and drink, and there may be a big party at the end. The *minga* is a Quechua tradition that has made its way into the mainstream of Ecuadorian society. A beach-cleaning campaign

will be promoted as a *minga* by an environmental organization, for example, as will any collective community action to improve local conditions.

DAILY LIFE

On the Equator there are twelve hours of daylight and twelve of darkness, and the rhythms of life in the country still follow the rise and fall of the sun. Ecuadorians will generally start the day with a hot drink. Herbal teas are popular in the highlands, and coffee more popular in the coastal lowlands, but many indigenous people still just start the day with a cup of hot water, believed to clean out the system. In the rain forests of Oriente, the local

Quechua have their own morning kick-start in the form of *guayusa*, a plant with caffeine-, vitamin-, and mineral-rich leaves, boiled to make a tea.

For the middle and upper classes, US-style breakfast cereals have become popular, but for the average rural farmer or urban laborer a heavy meal of rice, potatoes, and *menestras* (beans or lentils) is still the way to start the day. For office workers, a rushed breakfast at home might be supplemented with an *empanada* (a filled bread or pastry snack) or a crunchy, salted *tostado* (roasted maize) on the way to work. In the small towns of the Sierra, kids waiting for the school bus may sip on hot *morocho* (a thick, creamy combination of cracked corn kernels blended with milk, cinnamon, sugar, and raisins).

Schools start around 7:15 a.m. and offices at about 7:30 or 8:00 a.m., so early-morning buses and trams are packed with schoolkids in uniform and commuters. Offices break for lunch from about 12:00 noon, usually for an hour, though people stretch it to two hours when they can. With so many places offering a cheap *almuerzo* (two-course lunch with a fruit juice or drink), most workers will have lunch out a few days a week. In rural areas, shops might close until 3:00 p.m. for a little nap—a *siesta*.

Offices close about 6:00 p.m. The evening meal is normally eaten at home, with the whole family seated at the table, at about 7:00 p.m. to 9.00 p.m.

Everyday Shopping

The growth of huge US-style shopping malls in all the major cities of Ecuador and the rise of national supermarket chains have luckily not replaced the habit of shopping at the country's marvelous markets. Indigenous craft markets, like the internationally famous Saturday market in the Plaza de Ponchos in Otavalo, draw in tourists and locals looking for good-quality clothes and textiles, but the heart of most towns is the food market.

This is where the majority of Ecuadorians still shop for fresh fruit, vegetables, and meat. You can also have lunch there, enjoy a fresh fruit juice, and even pick up some herbal medicine or exorcise evil spirits. In Baños market, for example, you can visit a *curandera* for a healing whack on the back from a guinea pig, and then go outside and eat one of the little critters roasted on a stick (see page 95).

Everyday shopping is still done as it might be in a small town, in a *tienda de abarrotes* (grocery store), also sometimes called a *tiendita* ("little shop"); basically, these are the mom-and-pop corner stores close to home that stock a little of everything. Every town and village in Ecuador will have at least one *tiendita*, a *licorería* (liquor store), and a *farmacía* (pharmacy), and larger towns will have a dedicated *panadería* (bakery). Street stands are also a very important aspect of the informal economy, selling everything from hot snacks to fresh produce, clothes, fashion accessories, and pirated CDs and DVDs of the latest music and movies. There are several supermarket chains, including Aki, Supermaxi, and Mi Comisariato. They stock all the things you would find at home, although high import taxes make US imports expensive compared to locally produced alternatives.

Shopping malls have sprung up all over the country. The three-story Quicentro in Quito is enormous, with foreign clothing stores hawking goods at considerably higher prices than they do at home. Under one roof you can find a supermarket, bookstore, drugstore, and food court, with a McDonalds and other foreign and national fast food chains to choose from. Quito, Guayaquil, Cuenca, and Salinas all have large, modern malls, many containing multiplex cinemas showing the latest movies.

THE CYCLE OF LIFE

For both rich and poor, there is a cycle of family life that follows the calendar of birthday celebrations, national holidays, and local festivities. Families also come together to celebrate the important milestones marked by the Catholic Church. The baptism of a baby, when it is given its Christian name, usually takes place soon after birth. First communion is typically undertaken in a group, with children aged from seven to twelve dressed in white, with white gloves and a white candle symbolizing purity. It follows a course of religious preparation and is an expression of faith in the Church. The final step is confirmation, when at fifteen or sixteen years old a child commits to becoming a full member of the Church.

Perhaps the biggest event for girls is the *quinceañera*, the party held when a girl turns fifteen, which is seen as a rite of passage into womanhood and is like a wedding crossed with a debutante ball.

Weddings

There are few festive occasions in Ecuador as joyous or as costly as a wedding. For the elite a wedding involves a number of parties and related events, including a civil wedding, a lavish church wedding, and a reception. This last takes the form of a dinner, music, and dancing, with men in rented tuxedos and women in ballgowns. Civil ceremonies take place before a justice of the peace either in the civil register offices or at home. Those who can afford to have a civil wedding at home decorate their house or apartment, invite their friends, and have a party after saying their vows and signing the book.

Although Ecuador is a Catholic country, divorce has been legal since 1909 and is not a complicated process. As children are given both paternal and maternal surnames, there is no real stigma nowadays in being the offspring of an unmarried couple.

chapter six

TIME OUT

Life revolves around food in a big way in Ecuador.
The profusion of street snacks, the hawkers on the
buses selling sweets and savories, the lines outside cafés
and restaurants at lunch times, and bustling markets
brimming with fresh produce all confirm the national
obsession with good food. As we have seen, Ecuadorians
also adore family life, and take every opportunity to get
together in their free time and enjoy a meal, celebrate a
birthday, or throw a big party. A busy calendar of public
holidays and Catholic festivals and feast days means the
average Ecuadorian has more family time than the two-
week summer vacation enjoyed by most Americans or
North Europeans. An Andean wedding can go on all day
and all night. A village *fiesta* can last a week and bankrupt
the person known as the *prioste w*ho is given the privilege
(and cost) of organizing it.

On weekends, people head for the parks, which are
always full of children's parties and picnics, or set out for
the beach or the mountains to make the most of a *puente*
(long weekend). In Quito, roads are closed off on Sundays
to create a cycle route that brings whole families out on
their bikes. Parks have jogging trails, sit-up benches, and
dip bars for an outdoor workout. Popular sports include
soccer, another national obsession, and *ecuavoley*, a truly
Ecuadorian version of volleyball, with its own rules. For
the less energetically minded, shopping malls are great
places for city folks to spend the day people-watching and

snacking on fast food at the food court, while up in the highlands the colorful markets encourage locals to dress up and socialize.

Music is an integral part of free time for Ecuadorians, from the haunting indigenous sounds of Andean panpipes to the deafening bash of brass bands at village *fiestas* or the electronic *cumbia* music called *chicha* that fuels parties in mountain villages and city parks alike. Latin pop, *salsa*, and reggaeton are hugely popular in clubs; surf resorts springing up on the coast have a laid-back reggae vibe.

FOOD AND DRINK

The difference between the highlands and the coast extends to food, with a predominance of pork, potatoes, and maize dishes in the Sierra, and fish, seafood, and plantains on the Costa. Popular dishes from the highlands include *hornado* (roast pork), which is sold from roadside vendors or market stands. It's typically served with *llapingachos* (mashed potato and cheese patties cooked on a griddle). *Fritada* is fried pork served with *llapingachos*, or fried *yuca* and *plátano* (plantain). In case you haven't had enough pork, try some *chicharron* (pork rinds). *Patacones* are unripe plantains fried, squashed flat, and fried again to produce thick chips. *Chifles* are thin slices of fried plantain served with soup. *Seco de chivo* is goat stew, typically served with rice and plantains.

Menestras are lentils or beans served with *carne* (beef) and rice. *Empanadas* are pastries or dough balls filled with cheese, beef, or chicken, and make good snacks. Ecuadorians like their food spicy and make *salsa de aji* (hot sauce) of varying degrees of fierceness from Serrano chilis. The hottest *aji* is made with red chilis, salt, lemon juice, oil, onions, and cilantro (coriander). In some places they add the juice of the *tomate de árbol* (tree tomato) and *chochos* (lupini beans).

Chochos—Approach With Caution
There is one staple part of the Andean diet that you should always approach with caution. Lupini beans (*Lupinus mutabilis*) are small, white beans known as *chochos* in Ecuador. High in protein and other nutrients, they are extremely popular, sold on the streets from buckets by indigenous vendors, and added to salads and sauces in upscale eateries. However, they are bitter and slightly toxic in their natural state, and must be soaked and boiled and soaked again for three days before they are fit for human consumption. While *chochos* bought in shops and served at restaurants are generally reliable, some street traders soak their beans in the river, and this can lead to stomach upsets.

Vegetarians and Vegans

Vegetarians have plenty of fruits, soups, vegetables, pizzas, pastas, and pastries to choose from in Ecuador, but should take care when ordering food. *Sin carne* means without beef, not without meat, and "*Soy vegetariano*" ("I'm a vegetarian") may not be understood in the highlands or the jungle, where people eat pretty much everything.

Crazy for *Cuy*

Fluffy pet or tasty snack? Ecuadorians in highland villages laugh when foreigners are squeamish about snacking on *cuy*, the local name for a guinea pig (*Cavia porcellus*). Guinea pigs have been eaten in the Andean region for some five thousand years, and provided a valuable source of protein at a time when the only other domesticated animals were llamas and alpacas. They breed at a fast rate and are highly nutritious. Typically kept in the kitchen, they run free, feeding on food scraps. They are a popular food at festivals and weddings, and grace the Christmas table in many a highland home. They are also used in traditional healing (see page 67).

Before being roasted whole on the barbecue the *cuy* is stretched out flat, its big buck teeth making it look quite strange. The skin is basted with fat, which gives it a golden color and a crispy texture, and the delicious meat tastes like a cross between chicken and rabbit. Restaurants in Quito, Cuenca, and Baños all serve *cuy*, but they are not cheap, and might cost as much as $20 for a whole one with potatoes. If you want a bargain, keep an eye out for them on market stands in the highlands. If you  just want a small portion to say you've tried it, ask for a leg—"*una pierna, por favor*"—otherwise you might be

honored with the *cabeza* (head) and have to nibble
around those choppers.

When the Spanish conquistadors arrived in the
country they called these cute little critters *conejillos de
indias* ("little rabbits from the Indies") and brought them
back home, starting a craze for keeping them as pets. The
English queen, Elizabeth I, famously kept guinea pigs.

Amazing Maize

The variety of ways that Ecuadorians eat maize (corn, or
Indian corn) is astonishing. It's toasted, boiled, popped,
ground to make a dough, fermented to produce a mildly
alcoholic beer, or boiled up for a hot milky drink. And
if you think popcorn is something you only eat at the
movies or while stretched out on a sofa, in Ecuador you
can enjoy it sprinkled on soups or as a side dish at lunch.
Recent archaeological discoveries show that popcorn—
known by the Quechua name *canguil*—was a key staple
of early Andean civilizations four thousand years ago.
Another ancient use of maize that's enjoyed today, eaten as
a side dish with soups and *ceviche* (spicy raw fish), is *maíz
tostado* (toasted maize kernels). These are often referred to
in English as corn nuts, because they are crunchy and
salty, like peanuts. *Chulpi* is like a *tostado*, but sweet.

Choclo (boiled corn on the cob) is a standard
ingredient of soup, adding a touch of sweetness. A great
favorite in the highlands is *mote* (hominy), a variety of

maize with large white
kernels that are peeled
by soaking in slaked
lime (calcium
hydroxide) and boiled
before being served
either alone or as an
accompaniment to pork
dishes like *hornado* or

fritada. A breakfast dish from Cuenca called *mote pillo*, consists of *mote* fried with onions, eggs, milk, and fresh cilantro or parsley. *Humitas* are made from ground maize mixed with different ingredients, particularly cheese, wrapped in a corn husk and steamed. They are popular as a breakfast dish or as an afternoon snack in the highlands. Variations include the bigger *tamales* (doughballs stuffed with chicken or fish and boiled in a banana leaf), which are eaten at Christmas,

Evidence of boiling and fermenting maize to make a weak beer known as *chicha* has been found in the ancient Valdivia culture of the coast, and probably goes back much earlier. When Atahualpa had his first meeting with Pizarro's emissaries he served the Spanish conquistadors a special *chicha* made by the *acllas*, or Virgins of the Sun. *Chicha* beer is still the accepted payment for the communal work in the highlands known as *minga*. *Chicha* beer is such an important element of Andean civilization that there are several festivals in honor of it. The Festivales de La Jora in Cotacachi and the Yamor Festival in Otavalo celebrate the maize harvest and the days leading up to the solar equinox on September 22. The *chicha* beer served in Yamor is made from seven varieties of maize, including black, yellow, white, *chulpi*, *mote*, and *jora*. *Chicha morada*, or *colada morada*, is an unfermented version of *chicha* beer made from purple maize and fruits like *piña* (pineapple), *frutilla* (strawberry) and *mora* (blackberry). As we have seen, families take *colada morada* to cemeteries as a gift for their ancestors during the celebrations of the Day of the Dead. A sweet, creamy drink called *morocho* is made from boiling milk and maize flour with cinnamon and *panela* (unrefined sugar).

Soup

Hearty soups are a key part of any *almuerzo* (lunch), and are served with an unusual range of side dishes such as sliced avocado, *canguil* (popcorn), *tostado* (corn nuts), *arroz* (rice), *patacones* (plantain chips), and even *chicharron* (pork rinds). The most famous soup is *locro*, a thick potato soup containing chunks of cheese. *Yaguar locro* is potato soup with blood sausage. *Encebollado de atún* is a fish stew made with tuna, onions, tomatoes, and cassava, that is eaten for breakfast in many places and prized as a hangover cure. *Caldos* are more like broth, and include *caldo de patas* (cow heel soup) and *caldo de gallina* (chicken soup). *Guatita* is a hangover cure made from cow tripe. The one that makes me nervous is *caldo de nervio,* or *caldo de tronquito,* a stew made from chopped bull penis, that is sometimes sold as "natural Viagra" and is more popular than you might think.

Fish and Seafood

Along the coast and in the main cities, Ecuadorians enjoy a large choice of *pescado* (fish) such as *corvina* (sea bass), *pargo* (red snapper), *cherno* (grouper) and *picudo* (swordfish), usually served with *patacones* (thick plantain chips), rice, and a simple salad. In Esmeraldas the emblematic dish is a delicious *encocado de pescado* (fish cooked in coconut). *Ceviche* is a way of marinating fresh fish, or seafood with lemon juice and *aji* (peppers) that originates in the Andes. Shrimp must be boiled before

being marinated, but fish and seafood are effectively "cooked" in the citric acid of the lime. Before the Spanish brought limes from Europe, historians say *ceviches* may have been marinated in *chicha* beer. You can find *ceviche* made with *calamares* (squid), *pulpo* (octopus), *concha* (clams), *camarones* (shrimp), *langostinos* (jumbo shrimp), *erizos* (sea urchins), or *mixta* (mixed). The difference from *ceviche* in Peru is that in Ecuador they add tomato (even tomato ketchup) to the marinade.

Desserts

Ecuadorians have a sweet tooth and enjoy cakes, pastries, and desserts like *dulce de leche,* also known as *manjar de leche,* which is made from sweetened milk heated until it turns into a runny caramel. Other favorites are *dulce de higos con queso* (figs cooked in syrup served on soft white cheese), *quesillo* (crème caramel), *torta de zapallo* (pumpkin pie), and *quimbolitos* (sweet corn cakes with raisins). Fresh fruit prepared in a fruit salad is also typical, as are mousses made from *maracuyá* (passion fruit) and *guanábana* (soursop). *Helado de Paila* is a fruit sorbet from Ibarra that's made with sugar and egg whites.

EATING OUT

Ecuadorians love to eat out. In the main cities there's a wide range of restaurants to choose from, as well as fast food outlets, hole-in-the-wall eateries, markets, and street vendors. At the top end of the scale are places like Zazu in Quito serving fusion food aimed at businesspeople and the elite; in the middle are a profusion of Italian and other restaurants selling a variety of international dishes. Fast-food outlets like McDonalds, KFC, Domino's Pizza, and American Deli are considered middle class, and are located in the food courts of the biggest shopping malls, like the Quicentro in Quito, the Mall del Rio in Cuenca, and the massive Mall del Sol in Guayaquil.

The best value is found in places offering *almuerzo* (a cheap set lunch of two or three courses). This may include a juice, a hearty soup, meat, chicken, or fish with potatoes, rice, *menestras* (lentils) or *plátano* (plantain), and dessert. *Almuerzos* are served in restaurants or at covered markets. For many workers, this is the main meal of the day, and you find lines outside the popular places at lunch time. Set dinners, known as *meriendas*, are more expensive and not so popular, because less affluent Ecuadorians are more likely to have a meal at home with the family.

Chinese restaurants called *Chifas* are found all over the country. The two staples at *Chifas* are *chaulafan* (fried rice with chicken or shrimp or both) and *tallarines* (noodles). A very Ecuadorian snack sold from food carts is *salchipapas*, consisting of a portion of fries and a frankfurter drizzled in ketchup and served in a plastic bag. It doesn't sound very appetizing but tastes good after a night on the town. Drinkers in Cuenca, Baños, Guayaquil, and other places can soak up the alcohol with a late night *shawarma*, a pita

stuffed with spit-roast meat and falafel. On Sundays and special occasions like Father's Day it's typical to visit a *cevichería* for a plate of shrimp, fish, or seafood marinated in lemon juice and tomato. *Asaderos* specialize in rotisserie chicken; *parilladas* in barbecued meat, *chorizo* (pork sausages) and chicken; and *marisquerías* in seafood.

Drinks

One benefit of being on the Equator and having so many microclimates in one country is the abundance of exotic *jugos* (fruit juices) like *naranja* (orange), *piña* (pineapple), *frutilla* (strawberry), *mora* (blackberry), *maracuyá* (passion-fruit), *sandía* (watermelon), and *mango*. Some local fruits are seldom found outside the region, like the sharp but delicious *tomate de árbol* (tree tomato) and the creamy *chirimoya* (custard apple). In sugar-cane areas you can get *guarapo,* juice squeezed from the cane. Juices are sold in restaurants, cafés, markets, and street stands.

Water is not safe to drink from the tap. Some restaurants provide filtered water (*agua purificada*), but if in doubt buy bottled water, which is available everywhere.

Ecuador produces excellent coffee beans, but the best-quality coffee was always exported, leaving only instant coffee for local consumption. Luckily the situation has improved, and in some places you can now get good, freshly made coffee. The main chain selling coffee is Juan Valdez from Colombia.

Teas are very popular, and many Ecuadorians start the day with an infusion of *manzanilla* (chamomile), take oregano tea for an upset stomach, and prepare a refreshing cold drink called *horchata* from a cure-all mix of herbs. A jungle tea called *guayusa,* prepared for years by the Kichwa people of the Amazon, has high caffeine levels and is used in traditional healing. It is also added to homemade cane alcohol in some regions to produce a cocktail with an added kick.

Alcohol

Ecuadorians enjoy a cold *cerveza* (beer), although a limited range of lager beers can be bought at liquor stores, supermarkets, and little hole-in-the-wall corner shops in poor neighborhoods. The leading brand is Pilsener, a light, refreshing, good-value lager sold in small and large bottles. It is closely followed by Club Premium. Both brands are owned by the multinational beer giant SABMiller. A more recent entry to the market is the sweeter Brazilian beer Brahma, owned by the

Belgian-Brazilian multinational Anheuser-Busch InBev. Foreign beers such as Heineken and Guinness are stocked in some supermarkets and available at international hotel chains, but these are much more expensive, owing to the high taxes on imported goods.

In Quito a couple of microbreweries serve more adventurous beer options, such as Belgian ales and German-style dark beers. In Baños the La Cascada Brewery produces ales, porters and stouts for the Stray Dog Brewpub, and in Montañita you can sit in front of the surf sipping a pale ale, stout, or porter, thanks to the Montañita Brewing Company, owned by a local US expat. While Andean *chicha* beer is made from fermented maize and sugar (see above), down in the jungle regions it's made with cassava that's been chewed and spat out so that the saliva can aid the fermentation process. Best avoided.

Foreign spirits are very expensive, due to high taxes aimed at supporting local brands, and this has hit the whiskey market quite hard. Ecuadorians therefore drink local rum, which is good quality, or *aguardiente* ("firewater") a white sugar cane alcohol. Popular *aguardiente* brands are Cristal and Manabí. *Canelazo* is a hot mix of *aguardiente,* sugar, lemon, and cinnamon that is sure to keep the cold at bay on a chilly Andean evening.

Wine is taxed at a lower rate than spirits, but is still expensive compared to the USA or Europe, which is why you see so many cheaper but low-quality boxed wines on sale. Chilean and Argentine wines dominate the market, with sparkling wines favored at Christmas and New Year.

TIPPING

Giving a tip for good service is not compulsory in
Ecuador. Locals rarely add any extra to a restaurant
bill at an upscale eatery, which will already include an
added 10 percent service charge and 12 percent tax.

At informal places where you pay no tax there is no
need to tip, but most wait staff are low earners, so if
you've had good service you can show your
appreciation in the form of a dollar or two. Tip the
person directly; don't leave money on the table.

When taking a guided tour at a jungle lodge or in
the Galápagos, the usual rate for tipping guides is
anything from $5–$10 a day; you can give more or
less, depending on the service you receive. Don't
forget something for the driver or boat crew.

If you are driving, there's no need to tip gas
attendants unless they wash the windows and check
the tires—50 cents to a dollar is fine. If somebody is
watching your car for you, 50 cents is fine; tip them
when you leave.

At supermarkets there are often people who will
pack groceries and carry them to the car for 25 or
50 cents a bag. For a $7 haircut, if the barber does a
good job, a dollar tip is a good way to thank him.

SPORTS

Ecuadorians are soccer (football) mad. When the national
team, La Tri, is playing in an international match, especially
against Colombia or Peru, you'll find crowds cheering them
on in cafés and bars. For a small country, Ecuador has a
decent record in international matches over the last fifteen
years, qualifying for the World Cup in 2002 and reaching
the final sixteen in 2006 in Germany. Ecuador beat some of

the best teams in South America to qualify for the 2014 World Cup in Brazil, but never made it past the group stage, coming third behind France and Switzerland. The tournament was, however, a shop window for young players like Enner Valencia, snapped up by English club West Ham.

In May 2007 it looked as if Ecuador would be unable to host World Cup qualifying matches at its Atahualpa Stadium in Quito after FIFA introduced a ban on international matches at more than 8,200 feet (2,500 meters), FIFA president Sepp Blatter citing medical fears for the players and the alleged unfair advantage it gave the high-altitude host nations. A concerted campaign by Ecuador, Bolivia, Peru, and Colombia led to the ban being dropped in May 2008.

La Tri has benefited greatly from players gaining experience in Latin America and Europe. One of the big stars from the current crop of players is Antonio Valencia, who signed a multi-million-dollar contract in 2009 with English Premier League leaders Manchester United. Valencia is an example of how soccer can dramatically change the lives of Ecuadorians from humble backgrounds with a natural talent for the beautiful game.

While soccer is a national passion, Ecuador's national game has to be *ecuavoley*, a unique version of volleyball that pits three against three, is more relaxed on ball-holding than the European six-on-six or Brazilian two-on-two game, and has a higher net at 9.2 feet (2.8 m). The players are called the *servidor* (server), *ponedor* or *colocador* (setter), and *volador* (flyer), and the game is played with a

Chota Valley: A Soccer Factory

Ask any Ecuadorian where the best soccer players come from, and the answer will invariably be the Chota Valley in the northern provinces of Imbabura and Carchi, where a small but significant community of Afro–Ecuadorians lives, breathes, and sleeps soccer. The inhabitants of these dusty, valley-bottom towns are the second-largest black community in Ecuador after Esmeraldas. Descended from slaves brought from Africa in colonial times, they were organized in *huasipungos*, like the local indigenous groups, and put to work on sugar plantations. Today, Chotanos still maintain African drum music and dancing traditions, like *la bomba* and the bottle dance (where women dance with a bottle balanced on their heads). But it's their skill at the beautiful game that most defines the local people, and it's a source of great pride. Nowadays, half of the national team come from Chota and players who have had success in foreign leagues—like Ulises de la Cruz and Agustin Delgado, who both played for English teams—have been instrumental in turning round years of government neglect here by building schools, medical facilities, and, of course, soccer academies. Success in soccer has provided a way out of the local poverty trap for gifted young players and has acted as a partial antidote to the widespread racism and marginalization of black communities that was endemic in Ecuador until recently.

football on a hard concrete court. Teams play two sets of fifteen points each. The first local tourneys were set up in 1943 in Quito, where the first championship was played in 1958, and it has now spread to every corner of the country.

For those who can afford it there is an upscale country club scene, with immaculate courts and greens maintained at the swanky Quito Tennis and Golf Club.

   To encourage cycling, Quito's streets are closed on Sundays to create a long circuit from Parque La Carolina, through La Mariscal and Parque El Ejido up to Parque La Alameda and the old town. Bikes can be rented along the route if you want a workout, but be aware that the altitude can leave you breathless until you acclimatize. Mountain biking is popular in the highlands, with trails around

Baños and other mountain towns. For adrenalin junkies there's a white-knuckle ride down the slopes of Cotopaxi. Always check on recent seismic activity if planning an ascent of volcanoes. Road runners might prefer the Guayaquil Marathon, held on the first Sunday of October around the city's landmarks.

Sporting Legend

Ecuador's first and only Olympic medal winner is Jefferson Pérez, who won the 20 km Walk at the 1996 Atlanta Olympics when he was just twenty-two, becoming the youngest person ever to win the event. To the great delight of his fans in Ecuador, he picked up a silver medal twelve years later at the 2008 Beijing Olympics. Born in humble circumstances in the Cuenca neighborhood of El Vecino, Pérez sealed his international status and place in the record books after winning his third successive 20 km Walk World Championship in Osaka in 2007. He is seen as a role model for Ecuador's young athletes, and a national hero. The date of his 1996 Olympic victory, July 26, is now celebrated as Ecuador's National Sports Day.

Ecuador's year-round good weather and high waves have led to a growing surf scene. The 2013 ISA World Masters Surfing Championship was held in Montañita, and competitions have been held at Manta, Salinas, and Punta Carnero. You can even surf in San Cristóbal in the Galápagos Islands. The season is January through May, but you'll find surfers hanging out in Montañita all year-round.

CINEMA

Following the creation of the CNCine (Consejo Nacional de Cinematografia) in 2006, Ecuadorian film production has jumped to ten or eleven films a year since 2012. Directors to look out for are Cuenca-born Sebastian Cordero, whose 2011 film *Pescador* ("Fisherman") tells the tale of a fisherman whose unremarkable life takes a dramatic turn when he finds cocaine washed up on the beach. *Sin Otoño, Sin Primavera* ("No Autumn, No Spring"), a tale of teen rebellion and confusion that throbs along to the sound of the Guayaquil rock scene, was directed by Iván Mora Manzano. *A Tus Espaldas* ("Behind Your Back"), directed by Tito Jara, explores indigenous identity, class barriers, and racism in Quito. Leading the new wave is director Tania Hermida, whose 2006 movie *Qué Tan Lejos* ("How Much Farther?") won international awards, as did her 2011 follow-up *En Nombre de la Hija* ("In the Name of the Girl"). Hermida was instrumental in persuading DVD pirates to buy and sell legitimate versions of local movies by giving them access to discounted prices.

DVDs of Ecuadorian movies with English subtitles are on sale at the international airports in Quito and Guayaquil and offer an entertaining insight into the people and culture. You can find modern *multicines* (multiplexes) in large shopping malls in the big cities, but there are only 250 cinemas in total. English-language movies are shown either *doblado* (dubbed into Spanish) or *con subtitulos* (subtitled).

ART

Art is everywhere in Ecuador, from the pre-Columbian gold and ceramics on display in museums to the colorful textiles and tapestries woven today by the descendants of those first Ecuadorians. The collision of Spanish Catholic culture with traditional Andean and Inca culture led to a process of cultural *mestizaje* (mixing or fusion).

Colonial-era churches were built on the ruins of Inca temples as a way of showing who was in charge, but the profusion of gold leaf in places of worship echoes ancient Inca practices. So many churches, monasteries, and convents were built in the first years of the conquest that Spanish artisans couldn't keep up with the demand, and the Escuela Quiteña (Quito School) was founded at the Church of San Francisco. Here, indigenous painters and

carvers were trained to produce Catholic religious art for the Royal Audience of Quito until they surpassed their Spanish masters. For more than three hundred years, artists and craftsmen in Quito supplied artworks to the capital cities of Latin America and even exported to Europe, such was their fame. The exquisite baroque and rococo masterpieces of art and architecture found in Quito and Cuenca are among the best-preserved in Latin America, and it's easy to see why they were declared UNESCO World Heritage Sites. A good example of the cultural blending that defines the Quito School is the *Last Supper* in the Cathedral Church painted by Manuel Samaniego y Jaramillo (1767–1824). Instead of a Passover lamb on the table there's a roast *cuy*, and the disciples are drinking *chicha* and eating *humitas*.

Another star of the Quito School was the *mestizo* (mixed-race) artist Bernardo de Legarda (1700–73), who created the sculpture of *The Virgin of the Apocalypse* for the Church of San Francisco in 1734. Better known as *The Virgin of Quito*, or *The Dancing Virgin*, the small wooden sculpture shows a winged Virgin Mary, trampling on a dragon and beating it with a silver chain, that was inspired by a passage in the Book of Revelation. A 150-foot (46-meter) replica now stands atop the Panecillo, a hill that was sacred to the sun in Inca times. Designed by the Spanish artist Agustín de la Herrán Matorras, the iconic statue is made of seven thousand pieces of aluminum and was completed in 1976.

Following the Wars of Independence, artists like Antonio Salas (1780–1860) focused on portraiture of national heroes and patriotic scenes as the new nation sought to define itself. So-called *costumbrista* paintings by Joaquín Pinto (1842–1906), depicting local customs and everyday life, added to the nation-building drive. Modernism came to Ecuador in the 1930s with a strong influence from  the Mexican muralists and a determination to depict the plight of Ecuador's downtrodden and exploited indigenous population. Artists like Camilo Egas (1889–1962) and Eduardo Kingman (1913–98) led this move toward socially engaged *indigenismo* (indigenism), which was echoed in the writing of authors like Jorge Icaza in his most famous novel, *Huasipungo* (see page 112). Ecuador's greatest modern artist, Oswaldo Guayasamín (1919–99), was also inspired by the Mexican muralists and fired by a rage against the pain and suffering endured by the poor and the marginalized sectors of Ecuadorian society. The brilliance of Guayasamín lies in his combination of elements from Expressionism, Cubism, and pre-Columbian art to create a signature style that is instantly recognizable.

THE ART OF SUFFERING

Few painters are as instantly recognizable as Oswaldo Guayasamín. The twisted hands, screaming mouths, and haunted, emaciated faces of his mature work seem to fuse elements from Picasso's *Guernica* and the powerful depictions of saintly suffering captured by the Quito School painters into a moving portrayal of indigenous suffering in Ecuador and beyond.

Guayasamín was a champion of left-wing causes, and is famed for his portraits of Fidel Castro. In 1988, a mural he painted in Ecuador's Congress angered the US government because it showed a dark figure in a Nazi helmet with "CIA" written on it. Ironically, his international fame stems from the purchase of five of his works in 1942 by Nelson Rockefeller, which led to exhibitions in the USA. His final masterpiece was the Capilla del Hombre ("Chapel of Man"), a museum built to showcase giant murals of his work alongside his collections of pre-Columbian artifacts and art from the Quito School. It was finished in 2002, three years after his death. A quote on the wall of the chapel sums up his commitment to social causes: "I cried because I didn't have shoes until I saw a kid who didn't have feet."

MUSIC
Ecuador's diverse cultures are reflected in the many different genres of music you will hear as you travel around the country. Pan-Latin American rhythms and dances like *salsa*, *merengue*, Latin pop, and reggaeton are also popular, with an extra dose of reggae at surf spots along the coast.

The term *música nacional* ("national music") covers everything from pre-Inca tunes played on indigenous panpipes to Afro–Ecuadorian drum dancing, and a genre of sad songs known as *pasillos* made famous internationally by Julio Jaramillo (1935–78), whose birthday on October 1 is now celebrated as El Día del Pasillo Ecuatoriano (Day of the Ecuadorian Pasillo).

Highland *fiestas* swing to the beat of *sanjuanitos*, a genre of Andean dance music named after the San Juan Bautista festival on June 24, but which dates from Inca times and the Inti Raymi celebrations for the Sun God. *Sanjuanitos* are played on *bandolín* (mandolin), *charango* (a small ukulele made from an armadillo shell with two sets of five strings), guitar, and *bombo* drums. Bamboo flutes like the *quena*, *pingullo*, and the *rondador* (panpipes) give the music a haunting, melancholic edge. Once heard mainly in Otavalo and Imbabura Province, *sanjuanitos* are now popular at parties and *fiestas* across the highlands and in Quito. Electric guitar, bass, and Yamaha organ can be added to the mix, and it's not unusual to find a village brass band banging out *sanjuanitos* at a *fiesta* or wedding reception.

Afro–Ecuadorian music can be divided into two genres: *marimba* music in Esmeraldas, and *bomba* in Chota. The *marimba* is a percussion instrument with wooden bars that are struck with mallets. Native to West Africa, it is played like a xylophone and typically accompanies a large *bomba* drum, a *cununo*, which is like a tall bongo drum, and a *guasa*, a bamboo tube filled with seeds that is shaken. In Esmeraldas they dance the *bambuco* and *caderona* with African call-and-response vocals. Afro–Ecuadorian music in Chota has absorbed elements from indigenous Andean

music to produce a dance
called *bomba* that is played
on *bombo* drums and
guitars. Banda Mocho is
a Chota music institution,
keeping alive the
extraordinary tradition of
playing vegetables as if they
were brass band instruments

and leaves as if they were clarinets or trumpets. The *bomba*
is such a staple of Ecuadorian culture that *cumbia* bands
will play it at parties.

One feature of traveling by bus in Ecuador is the TV at
the front, playing music videos featuring scantily clad girl
bands with names like Grupo Deseo, Doble Sentido, and
Las Diablitas. These groups sing along to tinny *cumbia* and
salsa tracks played on a Yamaha organ and a metal scraper.
This type of *cumbia,* known as *chicha* or *cumbia chichera,* is
hugely popular and contains elements from Andean music.

LITERATURE

Ecuador's most renowned writer is the novelist and
playwright Jorge Icaza (1906–78), who achieved
international fame with his 1934 novel *Huasipungo*
(published in English as *The Villagers*). A masterpiece
of Latin American fiction, it tells the tragic tale of the
injustices and exploitation doled out to the indigenous
population of the highlands by rich and ruthless *patronos*
(landowners) in conjunction with a compliant and corrupt
Catholic Church and greedy foreign capitalists. The book
has been translated widely and sold millions of copies. No
other Ecuadorian writer has enjoyed such success, but the
local publishing scene is hampered by a small readership.

Contemporary author Gabriela Aleman has recently
bucked the trend with her 2007 novel *Poso Wells*, a tale of

criminals, call girls, and corrupt politicians set in the seedy underbelly of Guayaquil. Writers and poets who have helped to shape the country's sense of identity are Juan León Mera (1832–94), who wrote the national anthem, and liberal essayist and writer Juan Montalvo (1832–89), whose literary attack on dictatorship helped to bring down Gabriel García Moreno. After García Moreno was hacked and shot to death by a mob in Quito on August 6, 1875, Montalvo wrote: "It is My Pen that Killed Him!"

PLACES TO VISIT

Ecuador has so many great destinations to explore that it's impossible to see them all in one short visit, but the following is a list of a few of the must-see places.

The Galápagos Islands

Modern visitors to these remarkable volcanic islands can follow in the footsteps of Charles Darwin. Highlights include Darwin's famous finches, giant tortoises, blue-footed boobies, and marine iguanas. Snorkeling and diving are excellent, and you can swim with sea lions and penguins. It's the variety of landscapes and creatures on each island that makes them special, so a cruise is the best way to get the full Galápagos experience. Alternatively, base yourself in Santa Cruz and get a taste of island life between day trips to explore the rest of the archipelago.

Quito

Quito was declared the first UNESCO World Cultural Heritage Site in 1978. Founded on the ashes of the Inca Empire's northern capital by the Spanish conquistadors, it is the best-preserved colonial city in Latin America and one of the highest, at 9,350 feet (2,850 m). The narrow streets of the old town are like a living museum, with indigenous women in traditional highland dress, babies strapped to their backs, worshiping alongside sharp-suited career women at the fantastically gilded altars of baroque churches. Set in a valley dominated by the high peak of Pichincha volcano, Quito combines the historic churches, monasteries, and museums of the center with the vibrant restaurant and nightlife scene of New Town and La Mariscal. Quito is

also a good base from which to explore the rest of the country. Take a day trip to Mitad del Mundo ("Middle of the World"), a monument built to mark zero degrees, zero minutes, and zero seconds of latitude, where you can straddle the Equator, watch water spiral down a plughole in different directions depending on which side of the Equator you put the basin, and balance an egg on a nail.

Haggle for Alpaca Socks in Otavalo Market

The enterprising indigenous inhabitants of Otavalo, a highland town some three hours from Quito, have traveled the world with their alpaca sweaters, woolen ponchos, and hand-woven work. The local women wear the traditional full-length skirt, white blouse with flared sleeves decorated with woven flowers, hair in a braided ponytail, headscarf called a *fachalina*, gold beads, and red coral bracelets to ward off the evil eye. The men also have long ponytails and sport white trousers, ponchos, and felt hats. For the full experience, come here on a Saturday, when locals and tourists get to practice their haggling skills. For the best price try combining several items. The nearby town of Peguche is famous for woven tapestries and the workshop of master weaver José Cotacachi.

The Amazon Jungle

Known as El Oriente, the Ecuadorian Amazon follows the eastern border with Colombia and Peru and is one of the most ecologically diverse places on the planet. Not surprisingly, the bird-watching is world class, with twitchers (dedicated birdwatchers who travel long distances for their passion) checking off upwards of five hundred birds on their lists at some of the top jungle camps. You can also see monkeys, caymans, tarantulas, anacondas, and river dolphins, and fish for piranhas. Ecuador offers very reasonably priced jungle tours in a range of options from luxury camps such as Sacha Lodge to hammock-in-the-communal-hut experiences with tribes like the Waorani. The traditional starting points for jungle tours are Coca and Lago Agrio in the north, taking in the Cuyabeno Reserve, Napo River, and the Yasuni National Park. Tena and Puyo in the east also offer access to the Oriente, with the added bonus of adventure sports.

Baños

Just three and a half hours from Quito, Baños is a party town that has carved out a niche as the adventure capital of Ecuador and attracts a young crowd. Set in a warm valley blessed with natural hot springs—thanks to the volcanic activity that keeps nearby Tungurahua rumbling and occasionally erupting—Baños offers hiking, mountain biking, waterfall tours, and whitewater rafting. Or you could just switch off and steam in the local hot springs before dancing into the wee hours at one of the clubs along the strip.

The Devil's Nose Railway

The complete overhaul of Ecuador's Trans-Andean train line from Guayaquil to Quito is great news for railway fanatics or anybody who likes to sit back and enjoy the magnificent views along the famed Valley of the Volcanoes past the perfect cone of Cotopaxi. The Nariz del Diablo, or "Devil's Nose," is the jewel in the crown: a section of rail between the towns of Alausi and Sibambe that crosses over a sheer-sided mountain using a series of switchbacks. It's a tremendous feat of engineering, and offers spectacular views of the rugged Andean scenery.

Cotopaxi

You can easily visit the base of this imposing snow-capped volcano, as it's only an hour or so south of Quito, but the real rush comes from climbing to the summit. At 19,347 feet (5,897 m) Cotopaxi is the highest active volcano in Ecuador—although it hasn't erupted since 1942—and one of the highest in the world. Acclimatization is key to a successful ascent. It's best to take two days to reach the top, with a day of training to get the hang of crossing the glacier with crampons and ice-axe, an early night at the José F. Ribas Refuge at 15,748 feet (4,800 m), and then a very early 1:00 a.m. start for the five-hour trek to the summit. The reward of reaching the top includes a spectacular panorama and a view into the massive crater.

Colonial Cuenca

Ecuador's second UNESCO World Cultural Heritage Site and its third-largest city is filled with churches and historical monuments and steeped in colonial charm. More laid back than bustling Quito, Cuenca has been voted the number one retirement destination for US expats, for its year-round spring-like climate and interesting cafés, restaurants, and arts and crafts. This is a good place to visit local markets, see Panama hats made, and try a roast *cuy*. Once an important Inca town called Tomebamba, Cuenca is close to the important Cañar and Inca site of Ingapirca.

Pacific Beaches

From Esmeraldas in the north to Peru in the south, Ecuador's Pacific coastline includes a 528-mile (850 km) stretch of sandy beaches known as the Spondylus Route, after the seashells found in the ancient sites of the Valdivia culture. Closest to Quito are beaches such as Pedernales and Atacames, packed with partying locals on holidays and weekends. To escape the crowds, follow the coast to Mompiche or the island of Muisne. From Guayaquil the upmarket resort of Salinas is popular with those looking for nightlife and plenty of activities with their sun, sea, and sand. For a less developed resort, try the surfers' paradise of Montañita, a fishing village converted into a hippy hangout that swings to a Bob Marley reggae beat. The waves are big and can be "gnarly," so this is not the place for learners, but it's perfect for professionals, and international surf competitions have been staged here.

Much more developed is Bahia de Caraquez, about an hour north of Manta. South of Manta head for Puerto López and take a boat out to Isla de la Plata, in the Machalilla National Park. The sea here is a breeding ground for humpback whales from July to September, making it an excellent whale-watching spot, and you can see many birds and animals native to the Galápagos.

chapter seven

TRAVEL, HEALTH, & SAFETY

Ecuador has a good transport infrastructure and subsidized fuel prices. Travel within the country is cheaper than in the USA or Europe, easy to organize, and relatively safe. The locals love to point out that the country has such a wealth of diverse environments to explore that you could breakfast at a pristine beach on the Pacific coast, lunch in the lee of a snow-covered volcano in the high Andes, and dine in a jungle camp surrounded by rain forest and rare birds!

Healthcare is an important consideration. Prevention is better than cure, so ensure you have all the necessary inoculations before you travel, and take sensible precautions over food, drink, and exposure to the sun. Travel insurance is essential.

Ecuador has its fair share of pickpockets and scam artists, so it's important to take care of yourself and your belongings, particularly in the cities and when sightseeing or traveling at night. There are also some security hotspots along the Colombian border that should be avoided.

BY AIR

With airports in most major cities and towns, short flying times, and relatively low fares, traveling around Ecuador by plane is a good, safe option if you have limited time. The two major hubs for international flights are, not surprisingly, Quito and Guayaquil, and the flight between them takes an hour.

Quito's shiny new Mariscal Sucre International Airport in Tababela is about twenty-two miles (37 km) from the city center. There are planned road improvements that should cut the journey time.

The two airports in the Galápagos at Baltra and San Cristobal are served by flights from Guayaquil (an hour and a half) and Quito via Guayaquil (three hours). Rain forest tours in the northern Oriente start in Coca, which is just a forty-minute flight from Quito.

BY TRAIN

Significant recent investment in the country's rail network has spurred a real revival in rail travel, especially along the picturesque Avenue of the Volcanoes. The plan is to create a network of lines that will greatly increase the options available to travelers and reopen the historic route between Quito and Guayaquil. Sections of the old rail network are gradually being linked, and operations expanded from weekend services to four or five days on some routes. The days of carriages packed with woolly llamas, squeaking guinea pigs, and indigenous farmers taking their merchandise to market are long gone. Nowadays, the railway is run for tourists and steam train enthusiasts, and stations along the lines have been turned into mini museums of local culture, with craft displays and shows of local dancing.

In June 2013, for the first time in years, trains started to take passengers along the 280-mile Trans-Andean Railway from Guayaquil to Quito as part of a luxury four-day package known as the Tren Crucero. Passengers travel in carriages linked to steam and diesel trains along different sections of the track, sleeping in hotels, historic *posadas*, and eco-lodges along the way, with bus tours to sites of interest. The Tren Crucero currently operates twice a month, but tourists will soon have the option of taking a faster train service with more frequent departures on the Quito–Riobamba and Riobamba–Guayaquil lines.

For those looking for a shorter, cheaper taste of Andean train travel, the line from Quito's Eloy Alfaro Chimbacalle Station to Latacunga runs through the picturesque Avenue of the Volcanoes to the base of Cotopaxi on an *autoferro* (a diesel bus on rails)—a great way to take in the Andean scenery. Another route on the Riobamba–Urbina line takes you to the highest point of Ecuador's railway network. The station at Urbina at 11,824 feet (3,604 m) is the closest stop to Chimborazo, Ecuador's highest peak. Here, on the Tren del Hielo, you learn about the *hieleros* (ice men) of Chimborazo, who continue the tradition of cutting blocks of ice from the glaciers there, which they bring down by mule to Riobamba for use in fruit juices and *raspados*—a drink made of shaved ice and a flavored cordial.

The jewel in the crown for train buffs is the trip from Alausí to Sibambe that features switchbacks, perpendicular drops, and a real sense of the cutting-edge engineering (literally in some places) that was employed to get the train over the Nariz del Diablo, a nearly sheer mountain wall. Rather than going round or through the mountain, the US engineers employed a series of switchbacks, so the train first shunts forward, then the points are switched and it shunts backward, and so on, to zigzag its way up and down the mountain.

ON THE ROAD

An extensive program of infrastructure projects and road improvements, combined with a greater emphasis on enforcing traffic laws, has cut road journey times and made traveling safer than in years past. High mountain roads, poor signage, landslides, and mist and fog at altitude, however, still cause bus accidents, especially at night. In Quito, the number of cars and taxis on the roads lead to gridlock at peak hours, but a bus and trolleybus service with dedicated lanes and fixed bus stops helps to reduce travel times. Elsewhere, in the country, rules are more lax, and buses will still stop at any point along the road where passengers want to get off.

Taxis

With subsidized fuel and stiff competition for fares keeping journey prices low, taxis are a great way to travel in Ecuadorian cities, especially after dark, or when traveling to places where security is an issue. Taxis are easily identified on the streets: they are yellow and have orange license plates, unlike private cars, which have white plates. They also have a four-digit registration number on the front doors. Never get into an unlicensed taxi.

A typical ride within most towns and cities costs between $1 and $5, but drivers are known for inflating prices when they see a foreigner coming, so always negotiate a price before you get into the cab. At the main airports it's hard to get a good deal unless you leave the airport and hail a cab on the street, but considering the fare from Tababela International Airport to the center of town is only $25 or $30, for a distance of 22 miles (37 km), it's easier and safer to take an official airport taxi.

In Quito, Cuenca, and Guayaquil taxis are supposed to use meters, but only in Quito are the regulations strongly enforced. Even in Quito, if you're traveling early in the morning or late at night taxis will try to find an excuse for not using the meter, and will generally double daytime prices. Always clarify the situation with the meter before you start your journey.

In general, it is safer to have your hotel or a restaurant call you a taxi than to hail one on the street at night. In Guayaquil, where "express kidnappings" (see page 136) are more likely to occur, you should always call a taxi. You can also rent taxis by the day, if you plan a sightseeing trip that will take you out of town and don't want to take buses. This will work out at about $50 to $100 a day, which is more convenient than renting a car, and you won't have to negotiate the roads yourself.

City Buses

Quito, Guayaquil, and Cuenca all have efficient and cheap bus services, although gridlock at peak times can make progress slow, even with dedicated bus lanes, and pickpockets are a problem. In Quito, bus routes run along the north to south axis linking the popular hotel and bar district of Mariscal with the historic old town, for about 25 cents a journey. Make sure you have coins to pay with.

Alternatively, for the same price, with concessions for senior citizens, you can use one of the city's three relatively new urban transport systems: El Trole, Ecovia, and Metrobus. El Trole is a very efficient trolleybus system that runs for about eleven miles (18 km) from the north of the city to the main intercity bus terminal at Quitumbe in the south. With dedicated lanes linking the main stations along the north–south line, it is the fastest way to beat the traffic. Buses usually display their final destination on the front, but always ask the driver if he stops where you want to get off before you get on.

Intercity Buses

Each city and large town has its own *terminal terrestre,* with bus companies serving destinations all over the country. There are frequent departures on hundreds of buses of different levels of comfort, from chicken buses linking remote mountain towns to shiny, air-conditioned intercity buses with reclining seats and on-board entertainment. Bus terminals are generally clean and modern, with food vendors and bathroom facilities, but always take care of your belongings, as they may attract

pickpockets and bag snatchers. For short trips you can jump on a basic *buseta* (small bus with limited leg room and local stops), or you can buy tickets in advance for *buses de lujo* (luxury buses), which are more comfortable for long trips and will show a DVD en route (although expect some dire US shoot-em-up or inappropriate erotic thriller).

In smaller towns and villages there may be no bus station, and people will simply gather at a spot on the side of the road and wait for a bus to pass through. Ask locals where to stand and when the last bus comes through, as some buses will stop running in the afternoon and the only alternative could be a *camioneta* (see below) or an overnight stay.

For safety reasons it is better to travel in the daytime, as accidents and hold-ups are more likely to occur at night. Given the size of the country, journey times are relatively short to most destinations and prices tend to be no more than $1 an hour. A bus from Quito to Cuenca will take anything from eight to twelve hours and cost around $10 to $12. One from Quito to Baños takes about three and a half hours and costs about $3.50 to $4. Whatever the quality of the bus, expect itinerant hawkers to get on and launch into an elaborate sales pitch that far outstrips the value of the sweets, Korean ginseng capsules, or toenail clippers that they are trying to sell you.

Colorful Local Transport

In the beach resorts and fishing villages of the coast, you'll find fairly "homemade" cycle taxis (*bici-taxis*) and motorbike taxis (*moto-taxi*s) that are cheaper even than yellow cabs and can take up to four passengers. In rural areas where bus services are limited or nonexistent, *camionetas* (pickup trucks) operate as an informal bus or taxi service between towns and villages. They have no set schedules or stops and leave when full. Alternatively, if you are in a rush you can pay a set rate and leave when you like. Always try to ask locals how much they pay before you agree to a price with the driver. If not, you might be paying for the families that get in the back of the truck as you pull out of town. The most colorful way to travel is on one of the brightly decorated country and coastal buses known as *chivas* ("goats"), so-named because they were brought in to tackle steep mountain roads. They have bench seats that slat straight across the width of the bus with open doors at each end and are also sometimes called *escaleras* ("ladders") because of the ladders on the back of the bus that allow passengers to put their baggage, assorted merchandise, and livestock on the roof. The roof is also a great escape for passengers looking for respite from the crush of people squashed into the knee-numbing space between the benches. Increasingly common are *rancheras,* which are bench-

seat *chivas* mounted on a truck base instead of a bus base. In Quito and other places, there are city tours on *chivas* that can get very lively at night as the buses travel from venue to venue with live music, singing, dancing, and local hooch to get the party started on board.

Driving
Rental Cars
With gas prices so cheap and so many places to visit within a relatively short driving distance of Quito, Guayaquil, and Cuenca, you might want to rent a car from one of the many international or local car rental firms that operate at most airports. However, with taxis so cheap and driving conditions so different from those at home, you may prefer to pay a local driver to take you on day trips. This can avoid any problems if you have an accident, as Ecuadorian road rules are strict and drivers can be held in custody if there's any argument over who is responsible for a crash. If you do decide to rent a car you will need to be at least twenty-five years of age, have a valid driver's license (from your own country or an international license), and pay with a credit card. Read the contract carefully and factor in the extra taxes charged and insurance costs. Always check the brakes, seatbelts, and tires, and make sure there is a working car-jack (*gato*) and spare tire (*llanta de repuesto*). Note any dents with the rental agency before taking the car, and take photos of anything you might have difficulty explaining afterwards. Highways and city roads have improved greatly since President Correa launched major infrastructure work, but country roads can still be hit and miss and poor weather conditions can make driving difficult. There is no point in renting a car for city travel in Quito.

Rules of the Road

Ecuadorians drive on the right, as they do in the USA, but the driving experience is quite different and the rules of the road are only now starting to be strictly enforced. Drivers have to be both aggressive, to make progress in traffic, and defensive, as other drivers swerve around and cut in front of each other, overtake on both sides, and honk their horns impatiently. The situation is not helped in the main cities, where a horde of yellow taxis and motorbikes leads to gridlock at peak times.

Drivers and front-seat passengers must wear seat belts, and if you don't comply with this and are stopped by the traffic police, you'll be fined. There is a speed limit of 50 kmph (31 mph) in cities and 90 kmph (59 mph) on main roads. Slightly over the speed limit and you get a fine and six points on your license; significantly over and you get a hefty fine, ten points, and three days in jail.

Breathalysers (*alcoholímetros*) are increasingly being used at night to cut down on drunk driving. They take a photograph of the person being tested and are linked to a central computer that instantly provides a list of all previous infractions and license details.

Parking infractions can also lead to stiff fines and impounding of the vehicle, so always look out for a sign with a capital E with a diagonal slash through it, which stands for "*No Estacionar*" (No Parking). In Quito they have a system called *Zona Azul* (Blue Zone) with boxes marked in blue on the road. The idea is that you pay an attendant about forty cents an hour for a maximum stay of two hours, but very often they are not easy to find. Make sure you do find one, though, as vehicles that don't pay and display a ticket sold by the attendant are clamped and then towed to the Metropolitan Police pound.

PICO Y PLACA

The Pico y Placa ("Peak Hour and License Plate") program was introduced in May 2010 to try to reduce traffic congestion, encourage the use of public transport, and cut air pollution in the center of Quito in the morning and evening peak hours of 7:00–9:30 a.m. and 4:00–7:30 p.m. on weekdays. There are no restrictions on weekends or holidays. Basically, the last digit of the license plate determines the day of the week the vehicle is barred from the road. Only buses, taxis, and cars owned by seniors (people over sixty-five) and the disabled are exempt. The traffic police take this seriously, and to ignore it can prove costly. A first offense carries a $106 fine and the car is impounded for twenty-four hours; for a second offense the fine is $159 and the car is impounded for three days; and for a third offense it's $318 and the car is impounded for five days.

WHERE TO STAY

Ecuador offers all the usual accommodation options you would find in the USA or Europe, ranging from five-star hotels in the major cities to historic *haciendas* in the highlands, funky surf hangouts along the Pacific coast, or a hammock in the jungle, strung up under the stars.

In Quito and Guayaquil, business travelers have a

choice of international chain hotels such as Hilton, Best Western, Sheraton, and Marriot, with swimming pools, Wi-Fi, and all modern facilities. For more local color, head to the heart of the beautifully restored old town in Quito, where the five-star Casa Gangotena basks in Baroque splendor in Plaza San Francisco.

Boutique hotels offer a more intimate taste of luxury on a smaller budget. The quirky Mansión del Angel in Quito has four-poster beds and elegant colonial antiques and reproductions. In Cuenca you can stay at one of the classic hotels in the café and restaurant district of Barrancos, overlooking the Tomebamba River, or one of the little backpacker places known as *hostales*.

One of the greatest concentrations of accommodation options for tourists is in Baños, known as the adventure-sports capital of Ecuador and a party town. There's a *hostal* on nearly every corner, and plenty of boutique-style places for the more discerning traveler.

Out in the country, along the Avenue of the Volcanoes, you can stay in grand old *haciendas*. One of the most famous is San Agustín de Callo, built on the site of a former Inca palace with an unrivaled view of the snow-capped peak of Cotopaxi.

A range of jungle lodges offers rain forest tours from the basic, living-with-indigenous-tribes approach of the small-scale Huaorani Ecolodge on the Shiripuno River, to the luxury of hot showers, buffet blowouts, and expert bird-watching guides at Sacha Lodge, with its massive observation tower and canopy walks. A new place that breaks all the usual rules for eco-friendly rain forest retreats is the award-winning Mashpi Lodge. Located some three

hours from Quito in a private nature reserve in the Mindo area, Mashpi was built to compete with the best luxury boutique hotels in the world. Designed by Ecuadorian architect Alfredo Ribadeneira, the main hotel building is ultra-modern and minimalist, with sharp angles and ceiling-to-floor glass walls that contrast dramatically with the organic lushness of the cloud forest outside. Guests can watch hummingbirds feed on nectar as they dine in the chic dining area, and marvel at the low grunts of black howler monkeys as they luxuriate in their Philippe Starck bathtub.

If you want to stay overnight at the Cañari and Inca archaeological site at Ingapirca, the only option is the rustic Posada Ingapirca, which offers chalet-style rooms with log fires to keep out the evening chill.

In the Galápagos, visitors to one of the four inhabited islands can choose from a range of options, including luxury and mid-range hotels and budget-end *hosterías*. Most visitors take a cruise and sleep on board the boat as it travels between islands. At the top end of the scale, large cruise boats holding up to ninety passengers have AC, hot water, swimming pools, and an expert naturalist guide on board. At the bottom end, converted fishing boats hold five or six, sleeping in bunks, there's one shower for all, and your guide might have limited English. The two main islands for land-based tours are San Cristóbal and Santa Cruz. The Finch Bay Hotel in the Santa Cruz capital of Puerto Ayora is the top of the range in terms of comfort and facilities, and the only one facing its own sandy beach.

A popular and economical option for those seeking to immerse themselves in Ecuadorian culture, either to learn the language or to contribute to a volunteer program, is to live with a family. Homestays can be arranged through most language schools and offer the opportunity to practice Spanish and learn local expressions, eat home-cooked meals, and get to know your hosts. Homestays are usually offered in middle-class homes in Quito, Cuenca, and Guayaquil, but you can also arrange to stay with local families in Otavalo, where you can learn some Quechua, or with an indigenous family in the rain forest.

Accommodation prices in Ecuador increase during the *temporada alta* (high season), which includes Christmas, New Year, Carnaval, and Easter. For these periods, rooms at beach resorts or in cities and towns with popular festivals should be booked well in advance. For the Galápagos, the peak season for cruise boats coincides with the main US and European vacation periods from mid-June to early September, when schools are out, and over the Christmas and New Year periods.

HEALTH
Before You Travel
Ensure that you have adequate travel and health insurance to cover treatment in case of accident or illness. It pays to read the small print and find out what is and isn't covered, especially if you intend to go whitewater rafting in Puyo, horseback riding around Cotopaxi, or snorkeling in the Galápagos. The best policies cover you for emergency medical transport, evacuation, and repatriation. This is particularly useful if you plan to travel to the Galápagos Islands, where medical services are limited.

Have the required immunizations in good time before your departure. Shots for Typhoid, Hepatitis A, and Hepatitis B are recommended, and a tetanus-diphtheria booster if you haven't had one in the last ten years.

Pack long pants, shirts with long sleeves, and bug repellent, because in the rain forest the mosquitoes come out to bite as the sun is setting. You'll need sunhats and sunscreen. Traveler's diarrhea is common, so pack Lomotil or a similar product, which will help on flights or long bus journeys. Rehydration salts will also help.

On Arrival

Quito is the highest capital city in the world, and visitors who fly in feel some effects of altitude sickness, although generally these are only minor symptoms such as shortness of breath, dizziness, or drowsiness. The secret is to drink plenty of liquids and take things easy while the body acclimatizes. You should also avoid excessive alcohol intake, and swap coffee for one of the excellent herbal teas they drink up in the highlands, such as *manzanilla* (chamomile). In some hotels they will even provide a cup of hot coca tea, a traditional Andean remedy for *soroche,* or altitude sickness. If you experience more serious symptoms, such as headaches, nausea, or confusion, it is important to monitor the situation, but rehydration and rest will generally be enough to get you through the first day. If symptoms persist and get worse after two or three days you should see a doctor. There are some medications that are prescribed for altitude sickness, such as acetazolamide, but the simple act of descending to a lower altitude is the most effective response.

Take Precautions

Ecuador is a hot, tropical country with year-round sunshine, and as such visitors should take basic precautions when spending time in the sun. Sunburn is not just a problem at the beach or in the Galápagos, but in the mountains and the jungle as well. Some days may seem cool in Quito, due to its high altitude, but the sun can be fierce at midday and you should always wear sunscreen with a high protection factor and reapply it regularly while sightseeing. You should also drink plenty of liquids and wear a hat when out during the day to avoid sunstroke, especially on boat trips, where the sun is reflected off the water.

Tap water is not safe to drink. Many hotels and restaurants have filtered tap water, but when in doubt ask for bottled water, which is cheap and generally available. Avoid buying raw foods such as salads from street vendors. Diarrhea usually clears up on its own, and is just a reaction to a change in routine, new foods, and hot weather. The abundance of exotic fruits and fruit juices in Ecuador can sometimes lead to a loose bowel if you overdo it. The secret is to eat lightly, and keep up your fluid intake. Ecuadorians swear by *té de orégano* (oregano tea) for an upset stomach, which is very soothing. You will find it at most hotels and guesthouses if you ask.

Yellow fever is not a problem for visitors to the Galápagos, Guayaquil, coastal beaches, or the highlands, but vaccination is recommended for travelers to the jungle camps on the Amazonian tributaries of Oriente. A yellow fever certificate may be requested at the border if you are entering by land from Peru, so bring it with you.

Malaria is also confined to Ecuador's Amazonian jungles, and chloroquine tablets are recommended for those visiting lodges and camps, although you should consult the latest advice from a medical professional before taking medication. Other insect-borne diseases include dengue, a flu-like virus spread by day-biting *Aedes aegypti* mosquitoes. Known as breakbone fever (due to the pain felt in joints in extreme cases), there is no vaccination against it, so it is important to minimize insect bites by applying a repellent including DEET, wearing long sleeves and long pants after sunset, and sleeping under mosquito nets.

Healthcare

There is a two-tier health system in Ecuador: a public service that is free to all, funded from social security payments (under the Ecuador Social Security system, or IESS), and a private system. Big cities, like Quito, Guayaquil, and Cuenca offer excellent healthcare, with modern hospitals and clinics and well-qualified doctors, including specialists who have studied in the USA. Despite major investment in the public health system since 2008, facilities in remote areas can seem primitive by Western standards, and there can be long waiting times. The private healthcare sector offers sophisticated scans and lab tests, emergency facilities, plastic surgery, and all major operations for those who can afford it.

For minor ailments, many head first to the local *farmacía* (drugstore) to ask the pharmacist for advice. Most medicines and antibiotics that would need a prescription elsewhere are available over the counter. Pharmacists can also give injections. If it's late and your local drugstore is closed it will display a list of the closest pharmacies that are open. If a drugstore is open there is an illuminated sign on the front saying "*Turno*."

EMERGENCY NUMBERS	
Local Emergency:	911
National Police:	101
Fire Department:	102
Red Cross:	131

NATURAL HAZARDS

Ecuador is a land of high mountains and raging rivers, and in the rainy season, especially in unpredictable El Niño years, landslides and flooding are very real dangers. It is also one of the most volcanically active countries in South America with over thirty volcanoes, twenty-three of them active. Volcanoes can also affect major towns and cities. Tungurahua erupted on July 14, 2013, spewing ash as high as 33,000 feet (10 km) into the air, forcing the residents of Baños to evacuate and flights to be diverted. Tungurahua means "Throat of Fire" in Quechua, and is one of seven active volcanoes that have erupted since the 1930s. In 1993, after 339 years of inactivity, Guagua Pichincha, just seven miles (12 km) from Quito, belched a huge plume of steam and ash into the sky, forcing schools in the capital to close and residents to don masks. Recently, in June 2013, earth rumbles, blasts, and ash clouds from Reventador in the Amazonian province of Napo triggered a landslide that ruptured the Petroecuador pipeline in the region, causing an oil spill that reached Peru and Brazil. The chance of being caught up in a deadly eruption is slim, given today's sophisticated monitoring equipment and well-practiced evacuation measures, but hikers and climbers should always seek up-to-date advice about the status of a volcano before setting out. In Baños, residents are alerted to the risk of a major blast by sirens. If you should hear them, follow the yellow lines on the streets. They lead to evacuation shelters on the road to Puyo.

SAFETY

Crime levels in Ecuador are relatively low compared to Colombia and Peru, but visitors should exercise caution, especially in the first few days. Be particularly careful with your belongings when traveling by bus or taxi, when arriving at new destinations, and in crowded places like markets or festivals. Never carry anything you can't afford to lose or can't claim back on your insurance. At night, avoid public transport and ask somebody from your hotel to call a taxi stand. Don't flag a taxi down on the street.

There has been a rise in recent years of so-called "express kidnappings" (*secuestro express*), in which victims are held up at gunpoint or with a knife, robbed of their valuables, and taken to ATMs or banks and forced to empty their accounts before being released. Avoid being a target by traveling in a group, taking money out of ATMs in a bank during the day, and, again, calling a taxi service rather than hailing one. If you should be kidnapped, give your assailants what they want without a fight.

The main threats to tourists are petty opportunist crimes like pickpocketing or bag or camera snatching. This is especially true in the historic heart of Quito, the busy hotel, restaurant, and bar area of La Mariscal; the area around El Panecillo; and the El Ejido and La Cristina parks, although the presence of police on the streets of the old city makes it much safer to visit during the day.

Guayaquil has a reputation as the mugging capital of Ecuador, and the area around the docks is particularly unsafe. If taking city buses or the *trole* (tram), be aware that these get very crowded and provide a perfect environment for nimble-fingered pickpockets and bag snatchers. Carry only essentials and a "mugger's wallet" (see opposite). Strap a pouch or money belt under your clothes, split money into different pockets, and wear your daypack on your chest. Business travelers and tourists should always check the latest safety warnings from the Web site of their embassy or the US State Department.

Hot Spots to Avoid
Activity by left-wing FARC guerrillas, ex-paramilitary groups, and drug and crime gangs from Colombia make the border provinces of Carchi, Sucumbios, and northern Esmeraldas places to avoid unless you are using the main border crossing at Tulcan.

SAFETY TIPS

- Don't attract the attention of thieves. Leave gold chains, diamond rings, and expensive watches at home; keep cameras and cell phones out of sight.
- Don't use ATMs in the street or at night. Try to use the ones in banks during the day.
- Travel with others; you are safer in a group. Solo travelers, especially women, may be targeted.
- Learn some Spanish. The more you can speak and understand, the better.
- Listen to the locals. Heed advice on places to avoid, and don't enter poor areas of cities and towns.
- Know where you are going. Don't wander around with a map looking lost.
- Take taxis at night. Get the number of a reliable taxi company from your hotel and have them call you a cab. If you can't call, use the official yellow taxis with orange license plates.
- Avoid crowds. Don't travel on trams or buses with anything you mustn't lose, especially at peak hours.
- Use the hotel safe. Don't carry all your cash, but have something to hand over if you are mugged.
- Let it go. If you are held up by an armed assailant, hand over your stuff. Keep calm, and don't resist.
- Have a backup. Keep some bills hidden in your belt, shoes, etc., in case of emergency.
- Carry a "mugger's wallet"—a decoy wallet with a few small bills to use for minor purchases, an expired credit card, and a few old library or gym cards for credibility.
- Make copies of your documents. Scan your passport, airline ticket, and other documents, and e-mail yourself the copies, along with the relevant bank and credit card company numbers to phone and cancel cards in case of theft or loss.

BUSINESS BRIEFING

THE BUSINESS LANDSCAPE

Ecuador has benefited from a prolonged period of political stability, a strong economy, the adoption of the US dollar as its currency, and rising incomes, and there has been growing investment from foreign firms in all but the oil industry and mining, where state projects with China and Russia predominate.

Once dependent on the export of primary materials, notably cocoa, bananas, shrimp, and oil, Ecuador now has a growing manufacturing sector producing textiles and goods for local consumption. There have also been significant investments in infrastructure projects, such as the new airport serving Quito, and a major regeneration project in the historic heart of the city, which has also seen the opening of many high-end hotels and restaurants to cater to tourists and business travelers. A year-on-year increase in tourism has also given a

major impetus to tourism-related businesses in established destinations like the Galápagos Islands, and emerging destinations such as the beach resorts of the Pacific coast, jungle camps in El Oriente, and the towns along the route of the recently revamped train line between Guayaquil and Quito.

While much has been done in the last few years to cut back on red tape and modernize government systems for registering companies and submitting tax returns, changes to the operating agreements with foreign oil companies, higher tariffs on imports, and changes to labor laws have created some challenges for those doing business in Ecuador. The World Bank's 2014 "Ease of Doing Business Report" ranked Ecuador at 135 out of 183 countries, below India but above Bolivia, Haiti, and Venezuela. However, if you do your homework, make the right contacts, and find people to help you cut through the red tape and advise you on the legal regulations, Ecuador is a dynamic and vibrant market in which to do business.

As elsewhere in South America, whom you know is as important as what you have to sell, and putting the time into networking and face-to-face contact will be crucial to the success of any business venture. The key is to find people who can set up a meeting for you with decision makers or other important people in an organization, or get things moving if they stall. To ensure you meet the right people, start by consulting the business attaché in your country's consulate or make contact with local chambers of commerce (see below). Unless they come thoroughly recommended, avoid the many *tramitadores* (professional local fixers) who offer to cut through red tape, minimize the hold-ups for imports and exports, or set up bank accounts. Depending on the kind of business you plan to do in Ecuador, you'll need legal advice from a recognized local expert to produce and translate contracts.

Finally, you will need patience and flexibility, because locating the right people, organizing meetings, and dealing with delays and setbacks can be frustrating.

DOING BUSINESS WITH ECUADORIANS

Personal Relationships

Making a good impression, networking, and taking the time to get to know the right people are all very important in Ecuador, where family structures still dominate the business sector. Generally, Ecuadorians are risk-averse and like to operate in an environment where they know the person they are dealing with, especially in Quito, where old-school formalities are very much the order of the day. This is where the concept of *buena gente* (good people) comes in. If a potential business partner or customer believes you are a good person to do business with, then you have a better chance of sealing a deal. But getting to know people takes time, and foreign businesspeople eager to get things moving in Ecuador are often frustrated when initial meetings seem to revolve around social pleasantries—questions about your family, your hometown, and first impressions of Ecuador—rather than getting straight down to business. This is normal. Once a good relationship has been established things will start to move, but not as fast, perhaps, as in the USA or the UK. The key to networking is to meet people who can help you meet others, and make contact with company chiefs and decision makers whom you would otherwise find it difficult to meet. You will also need to put in the time, maybe on multiple visits, before you see results and make the right contacts.

Dress Code

The dress code in Ecuador is quite formal at meetings and business-related social events. Men typically wear a dark business suit and tie, and it is not considered appropriate to wear a tie without a jacket, although Guayaquil is less formal than Cuenca and Quito. It's not

generally acceptable to remove your jacket once seated, but if your hosts do so then feel free to follow suit. Women should wear a businesslike dress, or a skirt or trousers with blouse and jacket, and should look well groomed.

You should also dress professionally for a breakfast or lunch meeting, as Ecuadorians have high expectations of what you wear and will not be impressed if you turn up in jeans and a T-shirt. The same goes for evening events. Companies may invite you to dinner to continue to get to know you, so you should have at least one set of good clothes and shoes appropriate for a country club dinner.

WOMEN IN BUSINESS

Ecuador is still a macho country in many ways, but women are strongly represented in accounting, marketing, law, medicine, the media, and management, so you are in fact just as likely to find yourself doing business with a woman as with a man in Ecuador, and in this context you will find that women are seen as professionals, and foreign businesswomen will be treated with the same respect.

Natural entrepreneurs in a society where you have to work hard to make ends meet, women have traditionally been the backbone of the Ecuadorian economy. Many women take on two jobs to put their children through school, and in most offices there will be at least one with a sideline in cosmetics, dietary supplements, clothes, or Tupperware to supplement her monthly salary.

The only difference when meeting a woman in a business environment for the first time is to shake hands when introducing yourself. As for dress, business attire for women is much the same as in the USA or the UK.

ARRANGING MEETINGS

When dealing with government bodies the process of making an appointment is formal, bureaucratic, and sometimes very slow. Unless you have a direct contact, it is best to start with contacting your local Ecuadorian embassy by sending a formal letter in Spanish and then following up with an e-mail. If you can get the trade attaché at your embassy in Ecuador to help you with contacts, things will move faster. If you have Ecuadorian agents or partners, even better, as through them you will be able to set up a meeting in person.

With large businesses used to dealing with foreign companies, a direct e-mail in Spanish is acceptable for proposing dates for a meeting but it should be followed up by a phone call about two weeks before the meeting and another the day before to check that everything is on schedule. This might seem like overkill, but in Ecuador, where things can change quite quickly and where businesspeople are juggling many things at the same time, you need to keep in touch, gently remind people you're coming, and use the opportunity to build rapport.

Entrepreneurs who have spent months sending out e-mails from their home country without any concrete leads will find that once in Ecuador they will start to see progress. This is because Ecuadorians prefer to deal with people face-to-face, and once they know you personally will be more likely to introduce you to other business acquaintances and help set up meetings. If you want quick results you will have to come to Ecuador and meet people in person. Part of the challenge here, as in most places, is to grasp who has the power to do business and sign off on deals, and how you can arrange to meet them.

Timing

An important consideration when making appointments is that Ecuadorians take their weekends and holidays seriously. There is little chance of getting anything done on a Friday afternoon or during the long holiday periods, around Christmas/New Year, Carnaval, or Easter.

The best time for a meeting is in the morning. Depending on the size of the company, you may be invited to a breakfast or lunch meeting with several executives and decision makers. These often act as pre-meetings and a chance to find out more about you. Don't be frustrated if you don't get down to business straight away. This is not the time to get a decision.

Invitations

An invitation to dinner is probably prompted by the thought of your staying alone in a hotel in an unknown city rather than by a burning desire to do business with you then and there. The key thing is to remain professional at all times, even when out on the town, and remember that the etiquette in Ecuador is for the person issuing the invitation to pay the bill. Never offer to pay half the bill, as it will just look cheap. Offer to pay it all, but don't insist if refused, as this may cause offense. It's better to let your hosts pay, and for you to invite them for the next meal.

Punctuality

The unpredictable nature of traffic and a laid-back attitude to timekeeping by some Ecuadorians can result in a late start when it comes to meetings. A foreign businessperson should always arrive on time, although not before, and will need to factor in potential transport delays when making plans. If you do have to wait, even for an hour or so, or even reschedule the meeting for another day, this is nothing personal—it's just a local peculiarity that you will have to get used to. The important thing is not to get ruffled or show undue annoyance by last-minute changes, and to make sure you leave room in your schedule for such contingencies.

MEETINGS AND PRESENTATIONS

The formalities of a meeting usually begin with a greeting to the group of "*Buenos días*" ("Good morning") or "*Buenas tardes*" ("Good afternoon/evening"). Then you will be presented to each person in the room. It is typical to shake hands and use the expression "*Mucho gusto*" ("A great pleasure") or "*Es un placer conocerle*" ("It's a pleasure to meet you"). Bring business cards printed in English on one side and Spanish on the other. Any material or brochures you bring should also be translated into Spanish, preferably by a local translator to get the tone right and to avoid words with different meanings in different Spanish-speaking countries.

If your Spanish is not fluent, you will also need an interpreter or an intermediary or partner. Generally, senior executives in large private companies will speak English, but there is no guarantee, and junior executives with key expertise pertaining to any deal may have no English at all. When dealing with government agencies you should always bring a translator and have a document drawn up in Spanish with the main points of your proposal. Presentations should also be given in Spanish.

Questions may be asked in a very direct way, but don't take this as confrontational. Give calm, measured responses. Stay cool, friendly, and professional at all times. Don't be put off if there is conversation during your presentation, or if people take phone calls or leave the room while you are speaking; this is just another example of a more relaxed attitude to doing business.

NEGOTIATIONS

Having made your pitch and answered questions, don't expect an immediate answer. Several meetings will usually be needed before a deal is finalized. You will often be told that somebody else has to be consulted. When dealing with government agencies that is probably the case, but in private  firms this could also be a polite way of saying "We'll think about it and get back to you."

If negotiations drag on too long, however, it probably means that the Ecuadorian business is avoiding saying a straight "no" in favor of subtle hints. Having local contacts who are used to the subtleties of Ecuadorian negotiations will help interpret the responses you receive.

CONTRACTS AND LEGAL CONSIDERATIONS

Under the national constitution the government has the right to own certain industries that are considered "strategic", including those related to the oil and gas industry and the generation and distribution of electricity. With such a complicated and wide-ranging legal landscape it is advisable to seek guidance from a well-respected law firm on all the legal issues pertaining to any potential business venture before going ahead. Use a local lawyer and professional translator to draft contracts in Spanish and English and clarify any contractual issues before signing on the dotted line.

It's important to contact your embassy or business chamber for the latest updates on the legal status of foreign firms in Ecuador, as things are changing. Ecuador decided to leave the International Center for the Settlement of International Disputes (ICSID), for example, after an ICSID tribunal ruled that Ecuador should pay Occidental Petroleum $1.8 billion to settle a dispute over a contract with Occidental that Ecuador had annulled.

MANAGING DISAGREEMENT

If there is a disagreement over a contract or payment, the first and best option is to try to deal with it straight away. Good local legal advice is essential, as going to court over a contract breach can be a protracted and frustrating process. The Ecuadorian legal system is slow, judicial rulings can be unpredictable, and the judiciary not always impartial to external influences. The best way to avoid disputes is to maintain frequent contact with Ecuadorian business partners, which will help to build strong personal ties and flag issues before disputes arise. This may mean a closer working relationship than one would foster with a business partner in the USA or UK, and more time spent on the ground.

MANAGEMENT STYLE

Hierarchies are important in the Ecuadorian business environment, especially in the highlands, where formality and the use of titles is fairly widespread. "Sir" will appease most old-school superiors in the USA or UK, and in Ecuador it pays to know some of the usual terms employed when acknowledging the hierarchy of individuals in a company. These give insight into the pecking order in a company, and knowing them will certainly help if you are thinking of relocating, setting up a business, and employing Ecuadorians. It is typical for an engineer to be addressed as *Ingeniero* and a university graduate as *Licenciado* in the same way as a US employee would address a superior as "Sir." Foreign businesspeople are not expected to use these titles, but should be aware of them, and should use *Usted* (the formal singular form of "you") when speaking to senior executives.

A foreign businessperson managing Ecuadorian staff would be expected to act as a boss and maintain a certain distance while at the same time exhibiting enough empathy for them to be able to express their concerns.

DEALING WITH RED TAPE

Although the government has done much to increase transparency and reduce the amount of red tape involved when doing business in Ecuador, there have also been many changes over the last few years that have kept businesses on their toes as they try to catch up. These include filing tax returns, for example, which can now be done online, but instant fines are incurred if deadlines are missed. The rules on import/export have also undergone changes, and taxes increased on imported goods to favor locally produced goods. Labor regulations have also been tightened in favor of employees.

A trip to the bank to make a simple transaction can take some time if it involves foreign transfers, and visits to government offices can mean time-consuming and frustrating phone and e-mail communication, or hours waiting in line. One way to speed things up is to work with local partners, business associations, or reputable agencies that already have contacts and can cut down the time it takes to negotiate the necessary red tape. For importing or exporting goods through customs, a reputable local contact is essential, and local agents are a requirement for dealing with the government.

Useful Organizations

Foreign companies seeking to do business in Ecuador but lacking the advantage of good local connections should start by approaching the trade representative at their country's consulate who will be able to help with local advice and a list of reliable contacts and suggestions for business partners, agents, and legal representatives.

The US Embassy in Quito and the Consulate-General in Guayaquil have an Economic and Commercial Section that produces a regularly updated Country Commercial Guide aimed at assisting US companies and individuals interested in investing in Ecuador with information on the commercial landscape.

The UK Trade and Investment (UKTI) office based in the British Embassy in Quito helps UK businesses that want to export to or import from Ecuador.

Established business associations can provide information on the business climate and the market, and steer you toward reliable local partners and reputable legal firms. They include the Ecuadorian–American Chambers of Commerce and Industry in Quito, Guayaquil, Cuenca, Ambato, Manta, and Loja. There are Ecuadorian–British Chambers of Commerce and Industry (CICEB) in Quito, Cuenca, and Guayaquil.

Ecuadorian bodies such as Invest Ecuador also have useful information on specific investment areas being promoted by the state.

CORRUPTION

The government of Ecuador has taken steps to stamp out corruption by simplifying tasks like applying for visas and work permits and paying tax, and creating portals so they can be done online rather than in a crowded public office where a *tramitador* (agent) would charge to speed up the process by greasing palms. However, Ecuador still scores badly overall on Transparency International's Global Corruption Perceptions Index, coming in at 102 out of 177 countries in 2013, below Peru and Colombia, but above Bolivia and Venezuela.

Foreigners doing business in Ecuador should always steer clear of any individual or company that offers a shortcut to official procedures through any form of inducement, whether financial or in kind.

GIFT GIVING

When first meeting business acquaintances you are not expected to bring gifts, but something typical from your country can act as a good icebreaker. Most Ecuadorians have a sweet tooth, and a box of shortbread, fudge, or chocolates is very acceptable. Hefty taxes on imported spirits mean that high-end whiskey, bourbon, and vodka brands are something of a luxury in Ecuador, so a bottle of Black Label or Chivas Regal will generally be met with appreciation. It may seem obvious, but avoid giving Rolex watches or expensive gold and jewelry items, especially when bidding for contracts with government agencies, as this can give the wrong impression.

Once you get to know business contacts and build up a relationship you can make your choice of gifts more personal.

chapter nine

COMMUNICATING

LANGUAGE

The official language of Ecuador is Spanish, and more than 95 percent of the population speak it as their first language. There are some twelve indigenous languages, spoken mainly in the Sierra, the Amazon region of Oriente, and the coastal lowlands, and the vast majority of the people who speak them are also fluent in Spanish. A linguistic legacy of the Inca Empire is the prevalence of Quechua, the language of the Inca heartland in Peru that was imposed on the people conquered by the Incas and used as a *lingua franca* to aid communication. One of the distinctive features of the Spanish spoken in Quito and the Sierra is the use of many words borrowed from Quechua.

Ecuadorian Spanish

Ecuadorians will sometimes say that they speak *castellano* (Castilian Spanish), but that doesn't mean they sound like the inhabitants of central Spain and the old Kingdom of Castile. The term harkens back to the days of Columbus and the arrival of the conquistadors, who came from a collection of kingdoms, principalities, and independent territories that were not fully unified under the national banner of Spain until the eighteenth century. Variations in the Spanish spoken in Ecuador are linked to the evolution of the language over centuries of distance from Spain and interaction with the speakers of indigenous languages.

Ecuadorians, especially in Quito, speak slowly and clearly, with a pronunciation that is easy to understand if you have some basic Spanish. However, Ecuadorian Spanish sounds much softer than the Spanish you hear in Spain, and there's no use of the lisped "*c*" and "*z*" that in Spain makes *cerveza* sound like "thervetha."

People are known for their politeness in the Sierra, and there is a slightly deferential tone to the language in cities like Quito and Cuenca, which is reflected in the use of the formal pronoun *Usted* ("you," singular) rather than the informal *tú*. The use of this polite form extends to elders, authority figures, and anybody you meet for the first time, other than children. It is usual to stick to *Usted* until a closer bond is established. This shows respect and good manners, and will be noted as such. The best thing is to follow the cues of the person you're speaking to. If they switch to *tú*, you follow suit as it indicates a friendlier relationship, and one of equals. Ecuadorians don't use the informal plural *vosotros* ("you"), which is used in some other Latin American countries; they use *ustedes*.

Politeness is also evident in the use of diminutives, when -*ito* or -*ita* are added to the end of a noun to make it sound nicer. A taxi driver, for example, might say there's no need to use his *taxímetro* (meter) because the journey will cost "*Unos dolarcitos, no más!*" ("Only a few dollars!").

The people of Quito and the Sierra, known as *serranos*, can be identified by the use of Quechua words (see some below). In Guayaquil and on the coast people are louder and livelier, speak faster, and use more Colombian words, such as *bacán* and *pana* (friend). One thing you notice among male speakers is the use of a heavily aspirated "*s*" on some words, so that "whiskey" sounds like "wih-key," and "*no más*" sounds like "*no mah.*"

No More Confusion

Visitors to Ecuador are sometimes confused by the use of the expression "*no más*" (literally, "no more," or "that's all"), which Ecuadorians seem to use after every sentence, especially with instructions or suggestions. "*Sigue, no más*" is a way of asking you to move down the bus, and basically means "just keep going." Thus, the Ecuadorian song "*Baile, no más!*" translates as "Just dance!" or "Keep on dancing!" rather than being an exhortation to stop.

Spanglish

With the proliferation of English-language rock and pop songs on the radio, US TV shows on cable and terrestrial channels and the explosion of social media like Facebook and Twitter, it's not surprising that English words have slipped into the vocabulary of many young Ecuadorians. The Spanish word for parking a car is *estacionar*, but you often hear *parquear,* which is a hybrid of Spanish and English known as Spanglish. An Ecuadorian might say "*Me voy al mall para hacer shopping*" ("I'm going shopping in the mall"), or "*Necesito un job*" ("I need a job"). The popularity of social media has also led to expressions such as "*Dame un like*" ("Give me a like") or "*El O El*" ("LOL"). Another unusual crossover is the word *man*, which is used in its English sense except that it can also refer to women and has an unusual plural, *manes.* The result can be sentences like "*Esos dos manes no saben nada de futbol*" ("Those two guys know nothing about soccer").

Speaking Spanish

Almost every Ecuadorian child learns some English at school, but outside the hotels and resorts in areas popular with foreign tourists few people can say much more than a basic "How are you?" or "What is your name?" So the more Spanish you can pick up before you go, the better. Once you are in Ecuador, any attempt to speak Spanish will be met with appreciation, especially if you can use some basic Ecuadorian expressions. You'll be able to ask for things, understand the replies, and make meaningful contact with the people you meet. Using a few phrases like "*Sabroso, gracias!*" ("Tasty, thanks!"), to show your appreciation of food at dinner, or "*Chévere,*" meaning "cool" or "awesome," when asked what you think of Ecuador, will endear you to your hosts.

Those planning to stay longer will find good schools teaching Spanish in Quito, Guayaquil, Cuenca, many highland towns, and beach resorts. Many schools can arrange a home stay with an Ecuadorian family.

Other Languages

Of the twelve indigenous languages spoken in Ecuador, Quechua is the language group with the most speakers. It was brought to Ecuador by the Incas, and is known as Runa Simi (literally, "Language of the People"). Today, Quechua is spoken by more than ten million people from Colombia down to Argentina, making it the most widely spoken indigenous language in the Americas. The highest concentration of Quechua speakers is in Peru and Bolivia, where Quechua is recognized as an official language. In Ecuador, linguists have identified some nine variations of Quechua. Confusingly, Quechua-speakers in the Sierra often refer to their language (and themselves) as Quichua, while those in El Oriente prefer Kichwa, due to subtle differences in the languages that have evolved over time.

All of Ecuador's indigenous languages are classified as endangered, as they are not taught in schools and the indigenous communities have been broken up by labor migration .

A distinctive feature of the Spanish spoken in the Sierra is the widespread use of words from Highland Quechua. The pronunciation is the same as Spanish, so *guagua* sounds like "wa-wa" and *chuta* sounds like "choo-tah." *Ñaña* is pronounced "nya-nya" and saying "*Hola ñaño*" to a friend is like saying "Hi, bro."

Below are some of the most commonly used words from Quechua. Try them out with the people you meet on your travels, and your efforts to speak like a *serrano* will probably be welcomed with a smile. There are also a number of words and expressions that you will regularly hear in informal conversations in Ecuador.

SPEAK LIKE A SERRANO

Achachai	It's cold, freezing. (For really freezing, you can expand it to *achachachai*.)
Ararai	It's hot, burning
Atatay	Disgusting, horrible
Me cachas?	You get me? Do you understand?
Te cacho	I understand
Chompa	Light jacket
Chuchaki	Hangover
Chuta!	Wow!
Guagua	Child, baby
Guambra	Young man
Mushpa	Fool
Ñaño/Ñaña	Brother/Sister. Used toward friends in the sense of "bro/sis"
Shunsho	Foolish

SPEAK LIKE AN ECUADORIAN

Bacán	Great, excellent, cool
Buenaso	Great, excellent, cool
Cachos	Jokes
Chévere	Great, excellent, cool
Chiro	Broke. *Ando chiro* ("I have no money)
Choro	Thief
Farra	Party
Jeva	Girlfriend
Mono	Someone from Guayaquil
Pluto	Drunk. *Estoy pluto* ("I'm drunk")
Pana	Friend

ETIQUETTE

Having good manners and showing respect for others is very important in Ecuador. When entering a shop or office, or getting into an elevator, people will normally say to those present, "*Buenos días*" ("Good day") or "*buenas tardes*" ("Good afternoon").

Elderly people are treated with respect and addressed as *Señor/Señora*. In rural areas an elderly lady may be addressed as *Doña*. *Señorita* is the equivalent of "Miss" in English. If you don't know a woman's marital status, the best policy is to use *Señorita* with younger ladies and let them correct you. When being introduced it is customary to say "*Mucho gusto*" ("Very pleased") or "*Un placer*" ("It's a pleasure"), followed by your first name, unless it's a formal business setting, when you might say your full name and present a business card. In an informal setting men will shake hands as in the USA or Europe, but the etiquette between women, or a man and a woman, is a single kiss on the right cheek—just a touch and an air kiss.

In restaurants or at dinner it is customary to say *"Buen provecho"* ("Enjoy your meal") to other diners. When dining at home with an Ecuadorian family the meal may start with grace, and it is customary to bow your head while they give thanks to God for the food on the table.

BODY LANGUAGE

Nonverbal communication doesn't play as big a part in the lives of Ecuadorians as it does in, say, Cuba, Venezuela, or Argentina, where people talk with their hands and gestures can seem quite dramatic. In the Sierra people are more reserved with their body language, but they don't have the same narrow limits on their personal space as people in the USA or Europe. Even in the Sierra you will find people are tactile and will hug, kiss, and touch their friends and acquaintances. This is not a sexual thing. The kiss when greeting women is about showing friendship, and the backslap or hug when men meet is a gesture of closeness. On the coast and in Afro–Ecuadorian communities people are even less reserved, and body language is similar to that in other coastal communities in Latin America.

HUMOR

Ecuadorians' humor can be quite earthy, considering their reputation among other Spanish-speaking countries for being polite and reserved. They like to share a joke (*un cacho*) when in company. Most jokes are quite innocent, based on puns, but jokes about young women and homosexuals could come across as sexist—or at least as throwbacks to the 1970s—to visitors from abroad.

Strong regional rivalries mean that *serranos* and *costeños* make jokes about each other that are far from polite. The people of Tulcán are singled out for jokes that question their intelligence. TV comedy shows are still stuck in the Latin American macho mold, and rely heavily on stereotypes. Staples include good-looking girls in tight outfits parading around for the benefit of older men, bossy mothers-in-law, and wives with rolling pins waiting for a husband who comes home with lipstick on his collar. A popular character in comedies is a man whose wife controls him, known as a *mandarina*—a use of the verb *mandar* (to order) and the word for a mandarin orange.

Mother-in-Law Joke

"Yesterday two guys in the street shouted abuse at my mother-in-law." "Did you intervene?" "No, three people shouting abuse at her would have been too much."

Poor Pastuzos

Ecuadorians make jokes about people from the Ecuadorian border town of Tulcán, who are known as "*pastuzos*." "Why do *pastuzos* enter the market on their knees?" "Because they're looking for the lowest prices."

THE MEDIA

The Ecuadorian media landscape has changed considerably since President Correa came to power in 2007, with tighter media regulations, government takeovers of some media outlets, and legal action taken by the president against journalists and newspapers.

The measures have led some government critics and international press bodies to denounce what they call a crackdown on freedom of speech. The president has countered that some privately owned media organizations are "extremely corrupt, and extremely mediocre," and are run by powerful economic and political interest groups who for too long were able to print what they liked. Now, he says they will have to face the legal consequences if they publish defamatory, inflammatory, or erroneous reports aimed at undermining his government.

The situation came to a head in 2011, when President Correa sued the journalist Emilio Palacio for publishing an opinion piece in the newspaper *El Universo*, saying that the president was a "dictator" and had ordered the army to open fire on the hospital where he was briefly detained in

a de facto coup by disaffected police officers in October 2010. A court found Palacio guilty of defamation, and sentenced him and the newspaper's owners—Carlos, Cesar, and Nicolas Perez—to three years in jail, awarding the president $42 million in damages. The defendants subsequently fled to Miami, and Palacio was granted asylum in the US. President Correa said that he had won an important battle over a "media dictatorship," but, following criticism of the ruling by international press bodies, in 2012 he announced that he was issuing pardons for the four men and would not be pursuing the fines.

When the Wikileaks founder Julian Assange sought sanctuary in the Ecuadorian Embassy in London in June 2012 and was promptly offered political asylum, the issue of media freedom came under closer scrutiny. Some critics said it was hypocritical for the government to support a media freedom exponent abroad while cracking down on freedom of expression at home.

That criticism only increased after a new communications law was passed shortly after Correa's re-election in 2013. The new law saw the creation of a media regulating body with the power to impose fines, and new restrictions against "media lynching," and the publishing or broadcasting of material that could incite violence or racial or religious hatred. The result has been increased self-censorship by private media, an editor of *Hoy* newspaper saying that the media faces "a field full of land mines where no one can work with freedom and confidence." After thirty-two years of operation, on June 29 2014 *Hoy* suspended its daily print edition, citing a lack of advertising revenue and government pressure for the move. Government sources have insisted the new law restores "balance" in the media and is not a "gag law."

Newspapers

The most respected national dailies are the best-selling *El Universo* from Guayaquil, El Comercio from Quito, and the state-run *El Telégrafo*. *Hoy*, now an online paper, also publishes *MetroHoy*, Ecuador's first free daily, distributed on the trolleybus systems in Quito and Guayaquil. *Extra* is a sensationalist tabloid that serves up a daily diet of sport, sex, and crime. *Vistazo*, which is published in Guayaquil, is the most influential magazine in the country and has a good reputation for in-depth features covering current affairs and sports. All the major newspapers have Internet pages where you can read the news free of charge.

Television

Just as the state has acquired newspapers and radio stations under President Correa, public TV has also grown. The most popular state-owned TV channel is Ecuador TV, but the state has also acquired two private TV channels, TC Television and Gama TV, after their owners went bankrupt. One unusual feature on the state channels is President Correa's weekly TV show *Enlace Ciudadano* ("Citizen Link"), in which he discusses government programs, chats with guests, and even sings a few songs from different locations in the country. The two biggest private TV networks are Ecuavisa and Teleamazonas. They show a mix of studio-based lifestyle shows, Mexican, Colombian, and Venezuelan soap operas, local comedies, US series dubbed into Spanish, and news bulletins. Ecuavisa has had considerable success with the show *Ecuador Tiene Talento* ("Ecuador's Got Talent"). Teleamazonas has had several run-ins with the government over broadcasts deemed politically biased, and the owner was forced to sell off his shares in the channel to avoid legislation that came into force in 2008 banning people with banking interests from owning media outlets. There are several Cable TV companies, including the aptly named TV Cable, offering TV packages with English-language channels like HBO, Discovery, and Disney for a monthly subscription.

Radio

There are hundreds of radio stations broadcasting around the country, from large national private networks like Cadena Radial Ecuatoriana (CRE) and Radio Vision, with hubs in Guayaquil and Quito, to local village community stations broadcasting in Quechua. Radio is still the main source of news for many people, especially in remote areas out of the reach of TV and the Internet. You can even download Apps to your Smartphone that allow you to play Ecuadorian radio anywhere you have access to Wi-Fi.

Despite the popularity of *música nacional* in the country, the vast majority of the music played on the major stations is foreign-produced Latin pop and US chart music. Until recently you were more likely to hear a reggaeton by Prince Royce than a *cumbia* by a local artist and Ecuadorian music only made up about 5 to 10 percent of the total output on radio. That is all set to change under the new Communications Law that—in a bid to stimulate the local music industry—specifies that radio stations must dedicate half their air time to locally produced content. This is good news for the underground Guayaquil rock scene, and bands like Cadáver Exquisito and Niñosaurios, who featured in the 2012 movie *Sin Otoño, Sin Primavera* ("No Autumn, No Spring"). The new radio rules are also expected to boost sales of local artists like Paulina Aguirre, who won a Latin Grammy in 2012 for the Best Christian Album, the modern *pasillo* singer Juan Fernando Velasco, and the romantic pop balladeer Danilo Parra.

INTERNET

Ecuador has a growing number of Internet users, with about 43 percent of the population online at the end of 2012. That's not a massive number in comparison with the 66 percent of Internet users in Argentina, but it's still more than in Venezuela or Peru, and is not bad for a country in which many people still live in rural areas.

Overall, given the extreme nature of the country's geography, national Internet coverage is very good, with decent broadband speeds in the main towns and cities provided by a number of cable and satellite providers. Hotels and some bars also offer free Wi-Fi, especially in popular tourist resorts like Baños, Montañita, and the Galápagos Islands. In Quito, for example, the local authorities provide free Wi-Fi service in the city's many parks and plazas and at the bus station at Quitumbe. Where there is no Wi-Fi, you can generally find a cyber café offering a connection for 50 cents to US $1.50 an hour, even in smaller towns. In remote jungle areas and high mountain valleys, coverage can be sketchy or nonexistent. That situation is set to change, as Ecuador is shortly due to connect to a new submarine fiber optic cable that will increase speeds and capacity by up to 160 times its present levels. The mobile phone companies Claro, Movistar, and Allegro are also aggressively marketing Internet connection through their own networks.

TELEPHONE

A large part of Ecuador has no landline service due to the difficulty and the cost of laying copper cable connections to remote and high-altitude locations. The main provider of fixed landlines is the state-run phone company Corporación Nacional de Telecomunicaciones (CNT),

founded in 2010 as part of a government strategy to simplify the sector for consumers and implement a drive to improve coverage and services. CNT also took over the mobile phone company Alegro, to offer an alternative to the big two private companies Claro and Movistar, and now offers G4 telephony and mobile broadband. There is a choice of cell phone contracts offering Smartphone, with

Internet connection and Wi-Fi or pay-as-you-go options. There are stores selling phones and Sim cards in most shopping malls. Pay-as-you-go customers can add credit either by buying scratch cards, or electronically at newspaper kiosks, phone stores, and communication centers where the sign *recargas* ("recharges") is displayed.

To make calls without a mobile, head for the nearest *locutorio* (communications center). These stores usually have a few computers with headsets and webcams, so you can use Skype, and phone booths where you can make cheaper calls abroad than from a hotel.

MAIL

The national postal system, Correos del Ecuador, has offices in all major cities and towns and a distribution system covering the whole country and transfer abroad. Post Offices are open from Mondays to Saturdays from 7:30 a.m. to 7:30 p.m. There are no registered, certified, or priority mail options, and delivery can be slow, taking anything from a week or two to send or receive letters and parcels from the USA and longer for mail to Europe. More reliable are international courier companies, such as FedEx and DHL, which have offices in Ecuador's main cities. Whoever you use to receive parcels, be aware that the tax payable on imported goods is high and goods will not be released until it is paid.

CONCLUSION

First-time visitors to this small South American country are quickly won over by the warmth of the people and amazed by the incredible biodiversity, the world-class bird watching, and the variety of landscapes. Dramatic snow-capped volcanoes in the Andes, dense rain forests in the Amazon, historic cities, and unique island habitats off the coast are all packed into such a small space it is possible to experience the best Ecuador has to offer in one carefully planned visit and still leave enough for further exploration. As a consequence, tourism is booming, and US expats have been coming over in droves to make the most of the Equatorial weather, low cost of living, good healthcare, and dollarized economy.

Armed with the careful research outlined in this overview, we hope that tourists, business travelers, and those wishing to relocate here will now have the confidence to delve more deeply into this intriguing country and learn more about Ecuador's turbulent history, rich artistic and gastronomic traditions, linguistic quirks, and fascinating indigenous cultures.

Ecuador has evolved from a major cocoa and banana exporter to an oil nation that has to grapple with the environmental consequences of exploiting this important source of revenue. The largest reserves are located under the most biologically diverse areas of the rain forest, in the Yasuní National Park, and drilling will affect the wildlife and the indigenous Waorani people who live there.

After a period of extreme political unrest that saw governments fall like dominoes, President Rafael Correa's election in 2006 ushered in a period of stability, steady economic growth, and rising living standards. Ecuador is opening up in a way it has never done before, both socially and economically, and after the self-doubt of the difficult years, before and after dollarization, when over a million Ecuadorians left to build a life abroad, there is a new sense of optimism about the country's future.

Further Reading

Arana, Marie. *Bolivar: American Liberator*. New York: Simon & Schuster, 2013.

Brian, Kevin. *The Footloose American: Following the Hunter S. Thompson Trail Across South America*. New York: Broadway Books, 2014.

Darwin, Charles. *The Origin Of Species*. 150th Anniversary Edition. New York: Signet Classics, 2003.

Darwin, Charles. *Voyage of the Beagle*. New York: Dover Publications, 2011.

Grigsby Crawford. J. *The Gringo*. A Memoir. Washington: Wild Elephant Press, 2012.

Hemming, John. *The Conquest of the Incas*. Boston: Mariner Books, 2003.

Icaza, Jorge. *Huasipungo* ("The Villagers"). Carbondale: Southern Illinois University Press, 1964.

Jacobs, Michael. *Andes*. London: Granta, 2010.

MacQuarrie, Kim. *The Last Days of the Incas*. New York: Simon & Schuster, 2008.

Miller, Tom. *The Panama Hat Trail*. New York: National Geographic, 2001.

Nicholls, Henry. *The Galápagos: A Natural History*. New York: Basic Books, 2014.

Pearson, David L., and Les Beletsky. *Travellers' Wildlife Guides: Ecuador and the Galapagos Islands*. San Diego: Interlink Publishing Group, 2010.

Ridgely, Robert S., and Paul J. Greenfield. *The Birds of Ecuador: Field Guide*. New York: Cornell University Press, 2001.

Striffler, Steve, and Carlos de la Torre. *The Ecuador Reader: History, Culture, Politics*. Durham: Duke University Press Books, 2009.

Theroux, Paul. *The Old Patagonian Express: By Train Through the Americas*. Boston: Mariner Books, 1989.

Vonnegut, Kurt. *Galapagos: A Novel*. New York: Dial Press, 2009.

Whitaker, Robert. *The Mapmaker's Wife: A True Tale of Love, Murder, and Survival in the Amazon*. London: Delta, 2004.

Index

culture smart! ecuador

Acknowledgments

This book would not have been possible without the help and advice of many people in Ecuador. First and foremost is my good friend Digna Martinez, who gave me an invaluable insight into Ecuadorian life. I must also thank Monica Martinez Chicango, Jeannethe Chicango, Gabriela Naranjo, Samantha Tinsay, Katherine Shea, Dominic Hamilton of Metropolitan Touring, Guido Calderon of Monte Selva in Baños, and Florian Lasnes. This book is dedicated to my son Francisco and my wife Yadira.